Process Philosophy

Process Philosophy   A SURVEY OF BASIC ISSUES

Nicholas Rescher

UNIVERSITY OF PITTSBURGH PRESS

#45129221

CONTENTS

PREFACE

Process philosophy has interested me since I first encountered it in a seminar given by W. T. Stace at Princeton University in 1949—now over fifty years ago. This interest culminated in my book *Process Metaphysics: An Introduction to Process Philosophy* (Albany, N.Y.: SUNY Press, 1977). Over the years I have produced a series of papers and lectures dealing with various aspects of this topic. My objective in *Process Philosophy* has been to gather together these various discussions and blend them into a coordinated whole that both extends and rounds out the view of process philosophy presented in my earlier book.

As a philosopher deeply influenced by pragmatism, I have always felt that one of the best ways of appraising a philosophical thesis on theory is to ask whether it can clarify issues and solve problems. I put forward the present deliberations about process philosophy in this spirit—as an endeavor to illustrate through examples the sorts of benefits that the ideas of process philosophy can yield.

I am grateful to Estelle Burris for helping me to prepare this material for publication.

January 2000

Process Philosophy

CHAPTER ONE

The Promise of Process Philosophy

1. Historical Background

In recent years, "process philosophy" has become a catchphrase for the doctrines of Alfred North Whitehead and his followers. But, of course, this cannot really be what process philosophy is ultimately about; indeed, if a "philosophy" of process exists, it must pivot not on a *thinker* but on a *theory*. What is at issue must, in the end, be a philosophical position that has a life of its own, apart from any particular exposition or expositor.

Whitehead himself fixed on "process" as a central category of his philosophy because he viewed time and change as definitively central and salient metaphysical issues. Invoking the name of Henri Bergson, he adopted "Nature is a process" as a leading principle and saw temporality, historicity, change, and passage as fundamental facts to be reckoned with in our understanding of the world.[1] This view was underpinned by Whitehead's appreciation of Leibnizian *appetition*—the striving through which all things endeavor to bring new features to realization.[2] And beneath this lay the Heracleitean doctrine that "all things flow" and the rejection of a Parmenidean/Atomistic view that nature consists of the changeable interrelations among stable, unchanging units of existence.[3]

As Whitehead himself thus emphasized, process philosophy represents not a somehow personal position but a major tendency or line of thought that traces back through the history of philosophy to the days of the pre-Socratics. Its leading exponents were Heracleitus, Gottfried Wilhelm Leibniz, Bergson, C. S. Peirce, and William James—and it ultimately moved on to include Whitehead and his school (Charles Hartshorne, Paul Weiss) but also such other philosophers as Samuel Alexander and C. Lloyd Morgan.

As is often the case in philosophy, the position at issue is best understood in terms of what it opposes. From the time of Aristotle, Western metaphysics has had a marked bias in favor of *things*. Aristotle's insistence on the metaphysical centrality of ostensively indicatable objects (with *tode ti* as a pointable—at *this*) made an enduring and far-reaching impact. In fact, it does not stretch matters unduly to say that the Aristotelian view of the primacy of substance and its ramifications (see *Metaphysics* IV, 2, 10003b6–11)—with its focus on midsize physical objects on the order of a rock, tree, cat, or human being—have proved to be decisive for much of Western philosophy.

However, another variant line of thought was also current from the earliest times onward. After all, the concentration on perduring physical *things* as existents in nature slights the equally good claims of another ontological category, namely processes, events, occurrences—items better indicated by verbs than by nouns. Clearly, storms and heat waves are every bit as real as dogs and oranges. Even on the surface of it, verbs have as good a claim to reality as nouns. For process theorists, *becoming* is no less important than *being*—but rather the reverse. The phenomenology of change is stressed precisely because the difference between a museum and the real world of an ever-changing nature is to be seen as crucial to our understanding of reality.

Moreover, processes are not in general a matter of the doings of things. The fire's heat causes the water to boil. But it is clearly not a *thing*. To be sure, some events and processes relate to the doings or undergoings of things (the collapse of the bridge) or of people (Smith's learning a poem). Other events and processes relate to the coordinated doings of things (an eclipse of the sun) or of people (a traffic jam). But many events and processes are patently subjectless in that they do not consist of the doings of one or more personal or impersonal agents (a frost, for example, or a magnetic field). What is at work in these self-subsistent or subjectless processes are not "agents" but "forces." These can be diffusely located (the Hubble expansion of the universe) or lack any real location at all (the big bang).

The progenitor of this rival metaphysical tradition was Heracleitus. For him, reality is not a constellation of things at all, but one of processes. The fundamental "stuff" of the world is not material substance, but volatile flux, namely "fire," and all things are versions thereof *(puros tropai)*. Process is fundamental: the river is not an *object*, but a continuing flow; the sun is not a *thing*, but an enduring fire. Everything is a matter of process, of activity, of change *(panta rhei)*. Not stable things, but fundamental forces and the varied and fluctuating activities they manifest constitute the world. We must at all costs avoid the fallacy of materializing nature.

The principal standard bearer of this line of thought into the domain of modern philosophy was Leibniz, who maintained that all of the "things" that figure in our experience (animals alone grudgingly excepted) are mere phenomena and not really "substances" at all. The world in fact consists of clusters of processes he call *monads* (units), which are "centers of force" or bundles of activity. For Leibniz, processes rather than things furnish the basic materials of ontology.

Against this historical background, it seems sensible to understand "process philosophy" as a doctrine committed to, or at any rate inclined toward, certain basic propositions:

1. Time and change are among the principal categories of metaphysical understanding.

2. Process is a principal category of ontological description.

3. Processes are more fundamental, or at any rate not less fundamental, than things for the purposes of ontological theory.

4. Several, if not all, of the major elements of the ontological repertoire (God, Nature as a whole, persons, material sub-stances) are best understood in process terms.

5. Contingency, emergence, novelty, and creativity are among the fundamental categories of metaphysical understanding.

A process philosopher, then, is someone for whom temporality, activity, and change—of alteration, striving, passage, and novelty-emergence—are the cardinal factors for our understanding of the real. Ultimately, it is a question of priority—of viewing the time-bound aspects of the real as constituting its most characteristic and significant features. For the process philosopher, process has priority over product—both ontologically and epistemically. This process-oriented approach is thus historically too pervasive and systematically too significant to be restricted in its bearing to one particular philosopher and his school. Indeed, one cardinal task for the partisans of process at this particular juncture of philosophical history is to prevent the idea of "process philosophy" from being marginalized by limiting its bearing to the work and influence of any single individual or group.

2. Process Ontology

One way of downgrading processes is to question not their reality but rather their significance. On this perspective, it is conceded that nature is indeed replete with many and varied activities and processes but insisted that they are simply the doings of substantial agents and thereby secondary and derivative. Every verb must have a subject and every event or occurrence is a matter of the agency of things. Denying the ontological autonomy of processes, this process-reducibility doctrine insists that all there is in the world are things and their properties and actions. This position reasserts the orthodoxy that maintains the onto-logical substance bias of Western philosophy.

The fly in the ointment is that the world is full of processes that do not represent the actions of things (save on a rather naive and obsoles-cent atomist/materialistic model of nature). Although processes *can* be the doings of things, the idea that they *must* be so is nothing but an un-helpful prejudice. When water freezes or evaporates, it is not a "thing" (or collection thereof) that is active in producing this result. The "freshening" of the wind, the forming of waves in the water, the pounding of the surf, the erosion of the shoreline are all processes that are not really the machinations of identifiable "things." Consider such processes as "a fluctuation in the earth's magnetic field" and "a weak-ening of the sun's gravitational field." Clearly such processes will make an impact on things (magnetic needles, for example). But by no stretch of the imagination are these processes themselves the doings/activities of things/substances. There is not a *thing* "a magnetic field" or "a grav-itational field" that *does* something or *performs* certain actions—nor does the worth or sum *project* such a field. Where is the thing that is be-ing active when we have a fall in barometric pressure? For the process philosopher, the classical principle *operari sequitur esse* is reversed: his motto is *esse sequitur operari,* since being follows from operation be-cause what there is in the final analysis is the product of processes. As process philosophers see it, processes are basic and things derivative, because it takes a mental process (of separation) to extract "things" from the blooming buzzing confusion of the world's physical processes. Traditional metaphysics sees processes (such as the rod's snapping under the strain when bent sufficiently) as the manifestation of dis-positions (fragility), which must themselves be rooted in the stable properties of things. Process metaphysics involves an inversion of this perspective. It takes the line that the categorical properties of things are simply stable clusters of process-engendering dispositions.

But is the domain of process dispositions really free from the need for a rooting in the categorical properties of things? Is the dispositional realm autonomous—that is, can dispositions be self-activating? After all, dispositions are matters of if-then. If this is all we have, can we then *ever* move to the categorical sphere? The answer is affirmative. We can do this provided we have *nested* dispositions. If all we had were dispositions of the form "When and where p, there q," then, of course, we would need a categorical input (namely, p) to have a categorical output. But with nested dispositions of the form "When and where (when and where p, there q), there r" we can in fact get a categorical output from hypothetical inputs. Where dispositions are sufficiently complex (i.e., nested), a transition from the dispositional to the categorical sector is possible. Mere dispositions can combine to engender categorical actualities. And so processes (rod snappings) can occur in the framework of a process ontology that has no recourse to processual substances with categorical properties that ground or underwrite the dispositions (such as rod fragility) that processes actualize.

Thus one must not forget that even on the basis of an ontology of substance and property, dispositional properties are *epistemologically* fundamental. Without them, a thing is inert, undetectable, disconnected from the world's causal commerce and inherently unknowable. Our only epistemic access to the absolute properties of things is through inferential triangulation from their dispositional properties— or better from the processes through which these manifest themselves. Accordingly, a substance ontologist cannot get by without processes. If the ontologist's things are totally inert—if they *do* nothing—they are pointless and can neither act nor become known. For without processes, there is no access to dispositions; and without dispositional properties, substances lie outside our cognitive reach. One can only observe what things *do*—through their discernible effects—what they *are*, over and above this, is a matter of theory projected on this basis. And here process ontology cuts the Gordian knot. In its sight, things simply *are* what they *do*.

Processes can conceivably make do without things. (As the example "it is getting colder" shows, there can be "subjectless" processes—processes that, to all appearances, are not like sneezing or dissolving encompassed in the activities of things.) But no workable substance ontology can operate without a heavy reliance on processes. A substance, after all, is determined (individuated) as such by its properties, and there are just two major types here, namely the dispositional and the absolute (nondispositional, categorical). But the dispositional properties are crucial, at least from an epistemic point of view, for all that we can ever observe about a substance is what it does—what sorts of impacts (changes, effects) it produces in interaction with others—that is, the sorts of processes it engenders. The absolute (nondispositional) properties that we attribute to things are always the product of a theory-bound conjecture—features imputed to things to provide a causal explanation for their impacts upon others. As Leibniz insisted, a substance is primarily a center of force, a bundle of dispositions to exert impacts of various sorts upon the others. Substances can come upon the stage of consideration only through the mediation of processes.

A process ontology thus greatly simplifies matters. Instead of a two-tier reality that combines things with their inevitable coordinated processes, it settles for a one-tier ontology of process alone. It sees things not just as the *products* of processes (since one cannot avoid doing) but also as the *manifestations* of processes—as complex bundles of coordinated processes. It replaces the troublesome ontological dualism of *thing* and *activity* with an internally complex monism of activities of varying, potentially compounded sorts. If simplicity is an advantage, process ontology has a lot to offer.

3. Process and the "Problem of Universals"

Let us now turn from particulars to universals. Recourse to process is also a helpful device for dealing with the classical problem of universals. We are surrounded on all sides by instances of types of items more easily conceived of as processes than as substantial things—not only physical items like a magnetic field or an *aurora borealis* but also conceptual artifacts like words or letters of the alphabet, let alone songs, plays, or poems.

By their very nature as such, processes have patterns and periodicities that render them in principle repeatable. After all, to say that an item has a *structure* of some sort is to attribute to it something that other items can in principle also have.[4] But, of course, structure, though repeatable ("abstractable"), is itself not an abstraction—it is something that a concrete item concretely exhibits. Abstraction does not *create* structure but presupposes it.

Classically, there are three rival theories of "universals":

1. Universals are *made by minds* (nominalism): imputed to things by minds in virtue of their (the mind's) operation.
2. Universals are *found (by minds) in things* (Platonic realism): perceived by minds as preexisting aspects of things.
3. Universals are *generated in mind-thing interactions* (conceptualism).

Now a substance ontology, which is bound to see universals as simply being the properties of things (Aristotelian secondary substances), encounters serious difficulties here. For on its basis one is driven inexorably towards Platonism. We want universals to be objective but can only secure this status for them on the basis of a Platonic realism. And when we look more closely at the sorts of things at issue—letters of the alphabet, say, or poems—this option no longer seems to be attractive.

With process universals—conceived of as multiply instantiable processual structures—there are fewer difficulties. Processes are inherently universal and repeatable; to be a process is to be a process of a certain sort, a certain specifiable makeup. What concretizes processes is simply their spatiotemporal emplacement, their positioning in the framework of reality. A process as such is by its very nature a concrete universal—

any actual process is *at once* concrete and universal. There is, presumably, little or no problem about process types because these can be accounted for in terms of a commonality of structure. In particular, colors, say, or numbers, or poems lend themselves naturally to a process account. Take phenomenal colors, for example. A *mental* process such as perceiving or imagining a certain shade of red is simply a way of perceiving redly or imagining redly (in a certain particular way). A universal—for example, a phenomenal shade of red—ceases to be a mysterious *object* of some sort and becomes a specifiable feature of familiar processes (perceivings, imaginings). How distinct minds can perceive the same universal is now no more mysterious than how distinct autos can share the same speed. Otherwise mysterious-seeming universals such as odors or fears are simply shared structural features of mental processes. Universals are pulled down from the Platonic realm to become structural features of the ways in which we concretely conduct the business of thinking. Recourse to a process approach is once again a useful problem-solving device.

4. Process Philosophy of Nature

Let us now turn from matters of ontology to issues in the process philosophy of nature. A classical atomism whose ontology consists only of atoms and the void is the ultimate contrary to a process philosophy. A physics of fields and forces that operate on their own, without an embedding in things, is the quintessence of a process philosophy of nature. But wherein lies the appeal of such a view?

A substance-ontologist is committed to seeing the physical world (nature) as a collection of *things* and *objects*. And on this basis, one immediately faces the problem of accounting for *laws* that coordinate the behavior of things. (How do all hydrogen atoms learn how to behave like hydrogen atoms?) But by seeing the world as a matrix of process—by viewing nature as the substantiation of a family of operative principles (taken in their all-inclusive systemic totality)—we secure straightaway a coherent conceptualization of nature in a way that removes such difficulties. For the idea of law is inherent in the very concept of a process. And we can *understand* the world's processes—precisely because we ourselves are a party to them, seeing that we ourselves, in our own makeup and being, participate in the operation of nature.

A process approach thus simplifies greatly the problem of securing a coherent view of nature. Modern physics teaches us that at the level of the very small there are no ongoing *things* (substances, objects) at all in nature—no particulars with a continuing descriptive identity of their own. There are only patterns of process that exhibit stabilities. (The orbit-jump of an "electron" is not the mysterious transit of a well-defined physical object at all.) Only those stability waves of continuous process provide for any sort of continuity of existence. The development of stable "things" begins at the subsubmicroscopic level with a buzzing proliferation of "events" that have little if any fixed nature in themselves but only exist in reciprocal interaction with each other, and which have no stable characteristics in and of themselves but only come to exhibit spatiotemporally stable aspects at the level of statistical aggregates.

It was, in a way, unfortunate for the founding fathers of process philosophy that they did not witness the rise of quantum theory. The classical conception of an atom was predicated on the principle that "by definition, atoms cannot be cut up or broken into smaller parts," so that "atom splitting" was a contradiction in terms. The demise of classical atomism brought on by the dematerialization of physical matter brings much aid and comfort to a process-oriented metaphysics. Matter in the small, as contemporary physics concerns it, is not a Rutherfordian planetary system of particle-like objects but a collection of fluctuating processes organized into stable structures (insofar as there is indeed stability at all) by statistical regularities—that is, by regularities of comportment at the level of aggregate phenomena. Twentieth century physics has thus turned the tables on classical atomism. Instead of very small *things* (atoms) combining to produce standard processes (windstorms and such), modern physics envisions very small processes (quantum phenomena) combining to produce standard things (ordinary macro-objects) as a result of their modus operandi.

The quantum view of reality demolished the most substance-oriented of all ontologies—classical atomism. For it holds that, at the microlevel, what was usually deemed a physical *thing*, a stably perduring object, is itself no more than a statistical pattern, that is, a stability wave in a surging sea of process. Those so-called enduring "things" come about through the compilation of stabilities in statistical fluctuations—much like gusts of wind. Processes are not the machinations of stable things; things are the stability patterns of variable processes. All such perspectives of modern physics at the level of fundamentals dovetail smoothly into the traditional process approach.

Neither the logic of object and predicate nor even the grammar of subject and verb prevails in the language of nature; instead what prevails is the language of differential equations, the language of process. In this regard as in so many others, Leibniz had insight far beyond his time. Important though logic and language are (and he stresses that they are *very* important), it is the mathematical language of process—of transformation functions and differential equations—that is of the greatest help in depicting the world's physical realities. (This is something of which Whitehead, himself a first-rate mathematician, was keenly aware.)

5. Process Psychology: Difficulties of the Self

Next, let us briefly consider the utility of the process approach in philosophical psychology. The self or ego has always been a stumbling block for Western philosophy because of its resistance to accommodation within its favored framework of substance ontology. The idea that "the self" is a *thing* (substance) and that whatever takes place in "my mind" and "my thoughts" is a matter of the activity of a thing of a certain sort (a "mind" substance) is no more than a rather blatant sort of fiction—

a somewhat desperate effort to apply the thing paradigm to a range of phenomena that it just does not fit.

It feels uncomfortable to conceptualize *people* (persons) as *things* (substances)—oneself above all—because we resist flat-out identification with our bodies. Aristotle already bears witness to this difficulty of accommodating the self or soul into a substance metaphysic. It is, he tells us, the "substantial form," the *entelechy* of the body. But this accommodation strategy raises more problems than it solves, because the self or soul is so profoundly unlike the other sorts of entelechy examples that Aristotle is able to provide.

People instinctively dislike being described in thing-classificatory terms. As Jean-Paul Sartre somewhere indicates, a wrongdoer may be prepared to say "I did this or that act" but will resist saying "I am a thief" or "I am a murderer."[5] Such object-property attributions indicate a fixed nature that we naturally see as repugnant to ourselves. People generally incline to see themselves and their doings in processual terms as sources of teleological, agency-purposive activities geared to the satisfaction of needs and wants as they appear in the circumstances of the moment. In application to ourselves, at any rate, static thing-classifiers are naturally distasteful to us.

If one is committed to conceiving of a *person* within the framework of a classical thing-metaphysic, then one is going to be impelled inexorably toward the materialist view that the definitive facet of a person is the person's body and its doings. For of everything that appertains to us, it is clearly one's *body* that is most readily assimilated to the substance paradigm. Think here of David Hume's ventures into self-apprehension: "From what (experiential) impression could this idea (of *self*) be derived? This question is impossible to answer without a manifest contradiction and absurdity; and yet it is a question which must necessarily be answered, if we would have the idea of self pass for clear and intelligible. . . . For my part, when I enter most intimately into what I call *myself,* I always stumble on some particular perception or other, of heat or cold, light or shade, love or hatred, pain or pleasure. I never can catch *myself* at any time without a perception, and never can observe anything but the perception."[6] Here Hume is perfectly right. Any such quest for *observational* confrontation with a personal core substance, a self or ego that constitutes the particular person that one is, is destined to end in failure. The only "things" about ourselves we can get hold of *observationally* are the body and its activities.

However, from the angle of a process metaphysic, the situation has a rather different look. We have difficulties apprehending what we *are* but little difficulty experiencing what we *do*. Our bodily and mental activities lie open to experiential apprehension. There is no problem with experiential access to the processes and patterns of process that characterize us personally—our doings and undergoings, either individually or patterned into talents, skills, capabilities, traits, dispositions, habits, inclinations, and tendencies to action and inaction are, after all, what characteristically define a person as the individual he or she is. What makes my experience mine is not some peculiar qualitative character that it exhibits as the property of an object but simply its forming part of the overall ongoing process that defines and constitutes my life.

Once we conceptualize the core "self" of a person as a unified manifold of actual and potential process—of action and capacities, tendencies, and dispositions to action (both physical and psychical)—then we have a concept of personhood that renders the self or ego experientially accessible, seeing that experiencing itself simply *consists* of such processes. Based on a process-oriented approach, the self or ego (the constituting core of a person as such, that is, as the particular person he or she is) is simply a megaprocess—a *structured system of processes,* a cohesive and (relatively) stable center of agency. The unity of person is a unity of experience—the integrative coalescence of all of one's diverse micro-experience as part of one unified macro-process. (It is the same sort of unity of process that links each minute's level into a single overall journey.) The crux of this approach is the shift in orientation from substance to process—from a unity of hardware, of physical machinery, to a unity of software, of programming or mode of functioning.

Miguel de Unamuno says somewhere that Descartes got it backwards—that instead of *cogito, ergo sum res cogitans* it should be: *sum res cogitans, ergo cogito.*[7] But this is not so. Descartes' reversal of Scholasticism's traditional substantialist perspective is perfectly in order, based on the sound idea that activity comes first (*"Im Anfang war die Tat,"* as Goethe said)—that what we do defines what we are. The fundamentality of psychic process for the constitution of a self was put on the agenda of modern philosophy by Descartes.

Leibniz went even further in generalizing the view that agency defines the agent. Along Cartesian lines he saw the unity of the self as a unity of process, taking individuality to consist of a unified characteristic mode of acting (of perceiving the world). But in this regard the self was, for Leibniz, paradigmatic for substance in general. In effect, Leibniz's monadology took the Cartesian process approach to the personal self and *universalized* it to encompass substance in general. A substance, like a self, is just so much a "thing" as a center of action.

The salient advantage of this process-geared view of the self as an internally complex process of "leading a life (of a certain sort)"—with its natural division into a varied manifold of constituent subprocesses—is that it does away with the need for a mysterious and experientially inaccessible unifying substantial *object* (on the lines of Kant's "transcendental ego") to constitute a self out of the variety of its experiences. The unity of self comes to be seen as a unity of process—of one large megaprocess that encompasses many smaller ones in its makeup. Such an approach wholly rejects the thing-ontologists' view of a person as an *entity* existing separately from its actions, activities, and experiences. We arrive at a view of mind that dispenses with the Cartesian "ghost in the machine" and looks to the unity of mind as a unity of functioning—of *operation* rather than *operator.* A "self" is viewed not as a *thing* but as an integrated process.

On this basis, the Humean complaint—"One experiences feeling this and doing that, but one never experiences *oneself*"—is much like the complaint of the person who says "I see him picking up that brick, and mixing that batch of mortar, and troweling that brick into place, but I never see him building a wall." Even as "building the wall" just exactly is the complex process that is composed of those various activities, so—from the process point of view—one's self just is the complex process composed of those various physical and psychic experiences and actions in their systemic interrelationship.

The process-based approach in philosophical psychology doubtless has difficulties of its own. But they pale into insignificance compared with those of the traditional substantival approach.

6. Process Theology

Let us now move on to another theme, process theology.[8] The neo-Platonic sympathies of the Church Fathers impelled the theology of the Western monotheistic religions to the orthodox philosophical stance that to see God as existent we must conceive of him as a being, a *substance* of some (presumably very nonstandard) sort. To the pleasure of philosophers and the vexation of theologians, this has opened up a host of theoretical difficulties. For example: (1) On the classical conception of the matter, a substance must always originate from substances. Q: Whence God? A: From himself; he is *causa sui*. (2) Substances standardly have contingent properties. Q: Does God? A: No; he is in all respects (self) necessitated. (3) Substances standardly have spatiotemporal emplacement. Q: Does God? A: No; he, unlike standard substances, exists altogether outside place and time. And so on. No sooner has Western theology made God a substance in order to satisfy its ontological predilections than it has to break all the rules for substances and take away with one hand what it seemed to give us with the other. But in conceptualizing God in terms of a *process* that is at work in and beyond the world, we overcome many such difficulties with one blow. For it now becomes far easier to understand how God can be and be operative. To be sure, conceiving of God in process terms invokes recourse to various processes of a very special kind. But extraordinary (or even supranatural) *processes* pose far fewer difficulties than extraordinary (or let alone supranatural) *substances*. After all, many sorts of processes are, in their own way, unique—or, at any rate, very radically different from all others. It is not all that hard to see that processes like the creation of a world or the inauguration of its nomic structure are by their very nature bound to be unusual. But in the world of processes, that is not all that strange.

Moreover, there is now little difficulty in conceiving of God as a *person*. For once we have an account of personhood in process terms as a systemic complex of characteristic activities, and seeing God in these terms is no longer all that strange. If we processify the human person, then we can more readily conceive of the divine person in process terms as well. God can now be conceptualized as a complex system of characterized processes that creates and sustains the world and endows it with law, beauty (harmony and order), value, and meaning.

The process approach accordingly affords a framework for conceiving of God in a way that not only removes many of the difficulties inherent in the thing-oriented, substantial approach of traditional metaphysics but also makes it vastly easier to provide a philosophical rationale for the leading conceptions of Judeo-Christian religiosity.

7. The Agenda for Process Philosophy

As these deliberations indicate, the process approach has many assets. But it has some significant liabilities as well. For it is by no means unfair to the historical situation to say that process philosophy at present remains no more than a glint in the mind's eye of certain philosophers. A thoroughly worked-out, full-fledged development of this approach simply does not yet exist as an accomplished fact. All that we really have so far are suggestions, sketches, and expressions of confidence. The work of actually developing the process doctrine to the point where it can be compared with other major philosophical projects like materialism or absolute idealism still remains to be done. Many writers have hinted at a process philosophy, but nobody has yet fully developed one—not even Whitehead, though he has perhaps ventured further in this direction than anyone else.

Take just one example of the utility of the process approach. What is it that makes "*this* typing of AND" and "*that* typing of AND" two instances of the same process? Obviously, it is not the sameness of the product—otherwise indistinguishable ANDs can in principle be produced in very different ways by very different processes. Rather, structural identity of operation is the crux: the two concrete processes invoked are simply two different spatiotemporal instances of the same generic procedure—that is, that exactly the same recipe is followed in either case. But how such structures are to be characterized in general is far from clear. Clearly, the theory of process individuation and re-identification needs to be carefully developed. This issue is complicated because some ordinary language processes are in fact collected together as such not through processual sameness but merely through a sameness of product. Take Aristotle's example of "building a house." Clearly, housebuilding is not really a single sort of process at all but a family of processes linked only by a similarity of product. This sort of complexity needs to be taken into proper account.

Moreover, we require a more detailed theoretical analysis of the interrelationships of processes. It is clear, for example, that two such relationships are fundamental:

the process/subprocess relationship, which makes one process into a subsidiary component or constituent of another;

the concrete-process/process-type relationship, which joins two given concrete processes in a common type—presumably under the aegis of a principle of commonality of structure.

The character and connection between these modes of process relationship is something that very much needs to be clarified.

A good deal of work thus remains. To develop an adequate groundwork for process philosophy we need:

an analysis of the conception of process in its various manifestations and an explanation of which of its features have primary importance for metaphysical purposes;

a survey of the major sorts of processes that bear importantly in metaphysical issues;

a clear scheme for distinguishing the salient features of diverse processes: life versus inert, conscious versus unconscious;

a classifying taxonomy of processes of various sorts;

a reasoned schema for distinguishing and characterizing natural processes in a hierarchical format (protophysical, physical, chemical, biological, social) suitably distinguishing each level from and yet relating it to the next;

provision of a cogently developed line of argument for the primacy of process;

an integrated and coordinated presentation of the scientific and philosophical ideas relating to processes;

a thorough examination of the nature of such process-oriented conceptions as emergence, novelty, innovation, and creativity.

We do not as yet have any of these in fully developed form. Even if we did, they would only be the starting point. To provide an adequate account of process philosophy we need cogent and integrated expositions and arguments that articulate and substantiate the central theses of this position. Accordingly, a great deal of work remains to be done before process philosophy can become a well-defined philosophical doctrine. Perhaps, as Andrew J. Reck has noted, "the unfinished and never-to-be-finished quality of (processual) flux has seduced many adherents to the metaphysics of process among systematic theory-building."[9] Be that as it may, process philosophy at this stage of the historical dialectic is not so much a developed *doctrine* as a projected *program;* it is not an accomplished fact but a promising and, one hopes, developable project of research. True to itself, process philosophy is not a finished product but an ongoing project of inquiry.[10]

CHAPTER TWO

The Idea of Process

1. What Is a Process?

A process is an actual or possible occurrence that consists of an integrated series of connected developments unfolding in programmatic coordination: an orchestrated series of occurrences that are systematically linked to one another either causally or functionally. Such a process need not necessarily be a change in an individual thing or object but can simply relate to some aspect of the general "condition of things"— for example, a change in the temperature or in the purchasing power of money. A natural process by its very nature passes on to the future a construction made from the materials of the past. All processes have a developmental, forward-looking aspect. Each such process envisions some sector of the future and canalizes it into regions of possibility more restrained in range than would otherwise, in theory, be available. The inherent futurition of process is an exfoliation of the real by successively actualizing possibilities that are subsequently left behind as the process unfolds.

Processes develop over time: any particular natural process combines existence in the present with tentacles that reach into the past and the future. Just as there can be no instantaneous vibration or drought, so there is no instantaneous process. Even cognitive processes vary with the passage of time, as William James noted when he likened consciousness to "a bird's life; it seems to be made of an alternation of flights and perchings."[1] Moreover, processes will always involve a variety of subordinate processes and events, even as the process of creating a book involves its writing, production, and distribution.

Process is mereologically homogeneous: a part of a process is itself a process, even as a part of space is spatial or a part of time temporal. In this regard process is like physical substance in that a part of this sort of thing is itself a thing of the same general sort. Furthermore, not only do processes come connected, but so do their aspects. Even as in ordinary experience a person immediately focuses on only some feature of a larger complex whole, so in science we focus only on some features of the coherence we study and leave the others aside by an act of abstraction. Nature's processes stand connected with one another as integrated wholes—it is we who, for our own convenience, separate them into physical, chemical, biological, and psychological aspects.

A natural process is not a mere collection of sequential stages but inherently exhibits a structure of spatiotemporal continuity.[2] And just as the static complexity of a set of (filmstrip-like) photographs of a flying arrow does not adequately capture the arrow's dynamic motion, so the conjunctive complexity of a process's description does not adequately capture its transtemporal dynamics. Accordingly, the successive stages of a natural process are not a mere juxtaposition of arbitrary, unconnected factors (like passengers assembled by mere chance on a ship or plane). They are propositionally united by a systemic causal or functional agency under the aegis of a lawful regularity of some sort.

But how can a process preserve its own self-identity in the face of alteration—how it can be one single particular item and yet change? The answer lies in a single factor: internal complexity. A process does not change as such—as the particular overall process at issue—but will incorporate change through its unifying amalgamation of stages or phases (which may themselves be processes). Process philosophy has replaced a *horror vacui* with a *horror separationis;* being impelled by the paradoxes of Zeno into the conviction that once reality falls apart into disjointed discreteness, not all the king's horses and all the king's men can put it together again. (The "fuzzy" character of a reality without sharp boundaries, where things slide into each other by gentle transitions, is a key theme in Bergson and James.) The contribution of the process idea is to help us to keep together in reality things that thought inclines to separate in idea. These considerations indicate three pivotal facts:

1. A process is a complex of occurrences—a unity of distinct stages or phases; a process is always a matter of now this, now that.

2. This complex of occurrences has a certain temporal coherence and integrity, and processes accordingly have an ineliminably temporal dimension.

3. A process has a structure, a formal generic patterning of occurrence, through which its temporal phases exhibit a fixed format.

A process can be blocked by uncooperative occurrences. Things can go wrong and the normal unfolding of a process can be aborted through the intrusion of external events, such as when the germination and growth of an acorn into an oak tree is aborted through its being eaten by a passing pig or through the lack of something required for normal development (e.g., water or light).

Although processes themselves are always temporal, they can in general be given a temporal representation. Thus the mathematical process for solving an equation can be represented by a formalized instruction sequence, or a process of musical performance can be represented by the score that specifies how the performance is to go. Of course, such process representations are not themselves processes as such. The computer program for solving a mathematical problem is not a process—only its execution, carrying with it the actual solving of the problem, will be so. The program conveys the instructions by which a solver (human or mechanical agent) actualizes the process of producing a solution. Again the score of a piece of music conveys the instructions in line with which a process—the performance that realizes it—can be produced by players proceeding to do the appropriate things. The same holds true for the text script by which the human agents who function as performers can actualize the process of mounting a stage performance. In such instances, what we have is an instruction set, and these instructions do not constitute the process itself but merely the recipe to be followed by agents to produce it. In such cases, it is only the realization of the recipe—its concrete execution or realization—that constitutes a process (of solving or performing, respectively). But here —with such prescriptive processes—we are dealing with a special case. For the actualization of a process by an agent or agency must always intervene between the mere instructions and the fully realized process itself.

This line of consideration suggests that although the recipe or instruction set for process production is, or in a certain sense may be, timeless, the process itself must nevertheless be temporal. This means that processes can be said to exist only through their concrete historical manifestations. For processes, to be is to be exemplified. This means that the process must exist in time (with its full realization unfolding "in the course of time," so to speak). As long as it is not concretely realized, we have only a possible and not an actual process.

"But surely processes can be contemplated, thought of, described, and so on, without being exemplified." Quite right. But process descriptions (a conceptualization in general) do not *create* processes, any more than people descriptions create people. The principle "to be is to be describable" holds for process *conceptions* all right, but not for processes as such. The coherent *description* of a process does indeed indicate the existence of a correlative *process concept* in the realm of thought. But, of course, the process itself is something else again, something that must have its footing in space and time in order to exist. And a process is certainly not be identified with its usual product. Rather, structural identity of operation is the crux: the two concrete processes involved are simply two different spatiotemporal instantiations of what is generally the same modus operandi in that the same activities occur in either case.[3] The idea of process represents what might be called a *categorical* concept—one that provides a thought instrument for organizing our knowledge of the world.

A process is made into the item it is not, as with a classically conceived substance, through its continuing ("essential") properties, but by its history—that is, by the temporal structure of its descriptive unfolding across time. The identity of a process is constituted through its characteristic patterns of sequential occurrence. However, the programming of a process need not be totally deterministic; it can leave room for some degree of inner looseness, of variation and alternative possibilities. (A young girl's development through adolescence and puberty into adulthood is a definite process, but the specific course of development differs from individual to individual.)

2. Modes of Process

The basic idea of process involves the unfolding of a characterizing program through determinate stages. The concept of programmatic (rule-conforming) developments is definitive of the idea of process: the unity/identity of a process is the unity/identity of its program. But this unification can take different forms. If the "connection" at issue in that "sequence of *connected* developments" is one of actual causality, then we have a *physical* process; if it is a matter of mental or mathematical operations, then we have a different sort of process. However, our main focus here is on the physical processes in the natural world around us.

The issue of the typology of processes deserves attention. A *process* is a sequentially structured sequence of successive stages or phases that themselves are types of events or occurrences (in the case of an abstract process) or definite realization of such types (in the case of a concrete process). A structureless sequence—just one darn thing after another—is not a process. There are, accordingly, three principal ways of classifying processes: (1) by the character of the sequential structure at issue, (2) by the type of subject matter concerned in the way in which this character is realized, and (3) by the nature of the end result to which the process tends. Accordingly, the classification of processes will revolve around three questions:

1. What sort of structure?
2. What sort of occurrences?
3. What sort of result?

With respect to the first question, we can discriminate between different types of sequential structures, for example,

causal processes, such as seed germination, where each phase of development sets the stage for the causal production of the next;

thought-sequencing processes, such as instructions for parsing the grammar of a statement, performing long division, or extracting square roots. These processes take the form do this, then do this, then do this.

ceremonial processes, such as the king's toilette: first he removes his nightshirt and hands it to the master of the wardrobe, then he is helped into his undershirt, and so on.

performatory processes, such as the performance of a play or concerto.

With respect to the second question, we can discriminate between topical subject matter, for example,

biological processes
mathematical processes

mental processes

political processes

With respect to the third question, we can discriminate between different end results, for example,

productive processes whose end results are the realization of some sort of end products;

problem-resolving processes;

social-stylization processes, such as a wedding, coronation, or formal installation in office.

As the preceding deliberations indicate, processes at large can plausibly be classified in a tripartite schema: by structure type, by occurrence type, and by result type—that is, by format, by thematic content, and by end product. The key distinction between *productive* and *transformative* processes may be set out as follows:

Product-productive processes are those that engender actual products that can themselves be characterized as things (or substances); for example, manufacturing processes that produce pencils or automobiles and seed germinations that produce plants.

State-transformative processes are those that merely transform states of affairs in general, paving the way for further processes without issuing particular things or states thereof, for example, windstorms and earthquakes.

This distinction is important for present purposes because process philosophy is characterized by its insistence on the fundamentality of transformative processes, with their potential detachment from substantial things.

The distinction between *owned* and *unowned* processes also plays an important role in process philosophy. Owned processes are those that represent the activity of agents: the chirping of birds, the flowering of a bush, the rotting of a fallen tree. These processes are limited to particular substances that perform or undergo them. They relate to the doings of things. Unowned processes, by contrast, are free-floating and do not represent the doings of actual (i.e., more than nominal) agents: the cooling of the temperature, the change in climate, the flashing of lightning, the fluctuation of a magnetic field. From the process philosopher's point of view, the existence of unowned processes is particularly important because it shows that the realm of process as a whole is something additional to and separable from the realm of substantial things. With those agent-managed processes whose owners are intelligent beings there arises the question of the modus operandi—of the way in which the agent goes about engaging in this process. Moreover, the question of the object of the enterprise arises. Agent-managed processes are in general teleologically productive; they usually issue an *intended result* of some sort.

A process can be represented by a stable artifact: the poem recitation by the printed text, the musical performance by the printed score. However, it takes the intermediation of productive agents to turn such static process representations into actual processes. Taxonomically different sorts of processes can have the same kind of form or structure. Reading the poem to oneself is simply a process of information management. But reciting it or writing it down are processes that have a physical product. Yet these physical processes are isomorphic to the information-managing cognate: they have just the same processual structure.

One of the most important ways of classifying processes is through the thematic nature of the transformative operations at issue. On this basis we would have, for example, the distinction between processes of the following kinds:

physical causality (in relation to physical changes);

cognitive/epistemic (in relation to intellectual problem solving—e.g., programming ourselves for solving a certain sort of problem);

communicative (in relation to transmitting information).

Cognitive processes—procedures for solving various sorts of problems or answering various sorts of questions—are again of particular interest from the standpoint of process philosophy, seeing that they provide our only available access to understanding the world about us.

Although these processual distinctions do not exhaust the subject, they are among the most important in the domain. Yet classifying processes is a complex and diversified venture, and the present indications do no more than make a start, with the distinction between physical and mental processes playing a particularly important role.

3. The Complexity of Process

Processes are Janus-faced: they look in two directions at once—inward and outward. They form part of a wider (outer) structure but themselves have an inner structure of some characteristic sort, for a process generally consists of processes: microprocesses that combine to form macroprocesses. Process theorists often use organismic analogies to indicate this idea of different levels of units: smaller subordinate (or subsidiary) processes unite to form larger superordinate (or supersidiary) process units as cells combined into organs that constitute organisms. For some processists, this analogy is merely explanatory, for others it is a paradigmatic model revelatory of the deep nature of things. From either perspective, the idea of a hierarchic assemblage of micro-units becoming macro-units is a pervasive and characteristic aspect of process ontology.

Processes, after all, come in all sizes, from the submicroscopic to the cosmic. When smaller processes join to form larger ones, the relation is not simply one of part and whole but of productive contributory to aggregate result. The notes are not just constituent parts of the song, they are the active elements of its production. The fact that the unity of process is itself processual is enormously convenient for process philosophy because it means that no separate instrumentality of integration—process apart—is required to effect the identification of processes.

Processual particulars are themselves clusters of processes. Like an organism—a self-sustaining cluster of integrated processes (for nourishment, reproduction, and so on)—process particulars are systemic wholes comprising subordinate processes (in ways that proceed "all the way down" in such processists as Leibniz and Boscovich). It is thus for good reason that Whitehead characterizes his processual metaphysics as a philosophy of organism. For processists, organisms are if not the only natural particulars then, at any rate, paradigmatic instances. As Hegel already indicated, an organism is "a microcosm, the center of Nature which has achieved an existence for itself in which the whole of inorganic Nature is recapitulated and idealized."[4]

Whitehead makes much of a category he terms "nexus," which is designed to provide for the *combination* and *integration* of his atomic process units. A nexus represents "a particular fact of togetherness among actual entities," and reflects the fact that such entities make up organized groups or societies.[5] But in a way this is a needless complication forced on Whitehead by his commitment to process atomism of ultimately undissolvable processual units. Once this atomistic doctrine is abandoned, simplicity itself becomes the issue. Nothing is more natural than that miniprocesses should join and combine into macroprocesses, and a process metaphysic that does not commit itself to a Whiteheadean atomism needs no special machinery to accommodate this fact because it allows reality to be seen as processual "all the way down." A more satisfactory approach is thus reflected in the doctrine of "synechism" introduced under this name by C. S. Peirce, who defined it as "that tendency of philosophical thought which insists upon the idea of continuity as of prime importance in philosophy," with particular stress on the idea that "a true continuum is something whose possibilities of determination no multitude of individuals can exhaust."[6] In the end, individuality can be conceived of in terms of unity of process itself. The idea of process is thus a fertile device in ontology—one that is able to extend our informative horizons beyond the concept of substance that has historically monopolized attention in these discussions.

CHAPTER THREE

The Revolt against Process

1. Stage Setting

A contemporary review of W. V. Quine's 1960 book *Word and Object* of-fered the following observation:[1] "Even as Kant's search for 'the way the mind works' came up with the Aristotelian categories, so Quine's analysis of 'the way language works' comes up with object/subject and attribute/predicate linked by a timeless copula. Quine's view, like that of Aristotle, is atemporally object-oriented, and so he slights processes, temporal notions, verbs, and adverbs in favor of things, attributes, and timeless relations."[2]

In subsequent years it has become increasingly clear that the point of doctrine to which this review took exception, far from being somehow idiosyncratic with Quine, appears to represent the virtually standard position among recent writers on ontological subjects. The present dis-cussion is motivated largely by the (no doubt unduly optimistic) hope that we are here dealing with a tendency of thought whose rational cre-dentials are so *extremely* questionable that they are, at least to some ex-tent, effectively counteracted by the simple expedient of careful scru-tiny. (Perhaps this is somewhat unrealistic, since Quine's view of the matter bears the strap of orthodoxy, and orthodoxies, however prob-lematic, are not so easily dislodged.)

The ontological doctrine whose too readily granted credentials are here called into question consists of several connected tenets, the first fundamental, the rest derivative:

1. The appropriate paradigm for ontological discussion is a thing (most properly a physical object) that exhibits *qualities* (most properly of a timeless—i.e., either atemporally or temporally fixed—character).

2. Even *persons* and *agents* (i.e., "things" capable of action) are secondary and ontologically posterior to proper (i.e., inert or inertly regarded) *things*.

3. Change, process, and perhaps even time itself are consequently to be downgraded in ontological considerations to the point where their unimportance is so blatant that such subordination hardly warrants explicit defense. They may, without gross impropriety, be given short shrift in or even omitted from ontological discussions.

This combination of views, which puts the thing-quality paradigm at center stage and relegates the concept of process to some remote and obscure corner of the ontological warehouse, deserves to be characterized as a "revolt against process."

2. Manifestations of the Revolt

That we are actually witnessing such a revolt in contemporary philosophy is readily established. As already indicated, Quine's *Word and Object* took a position that squarely endorses the aforementioned tenets. The first chapter, entitled "Beginning with Ordinary Things," is devoted to maintaining that there is a basic orientation in language toward physical things—everyday material objects. Quine's position was admirably explicit: "Linguistically, and hence conceptually, the things in sharpest focus are the things that are public enough to be talked of publicly, common and conspicuous enough to be talked of often, and near enough to sense to be quickly identified and learned by name; it is to these that words apply first and foremost" (p. 1).

The index of Quine's book contains no mention of "process" or "change"; but process is in fact dealt with in a short paragraph (p. 171) in which it is thoroughly thingified. Quine's position is that "physical objects, conceived thus four-dimensionally in space-time, are not to be distinguished from events or, in the concrete sense of the term, processes." This thesis can, of course, be read in two ways. If x's are not to be distinguished from y's, then x's and y's are obviously of equal interest and importance. Instead, however, Quine uses the identification not as an occasion for equalizing the status of processes with that of things but as grounds for dismissing them from special consideration. Action and activity get short shift through Quine's endorsing "the idea of paraphrasing tensed sentences into terms of eternal relations of things to times" (p. 172). Time is in fact discussed at some length (particularly in sec. 36; but see also sec. 40); however, the discussion is premised on the thesis that Einstein's theory of relativity "leaves no reasonable alternative to treating time as spacelike" (p. 172). In sum, it is difficult to conceive of a more outspoken advocate of the subordination of processes to things than Quine. The fact that in this world things inevitably result from processes cuts little ice with him.

A second work that downplays process is Nelson Goodman's *Structure of Appearance*.[3] (I would exclude this interesting work from metaphysical purview if I felt more convinced that Goodman regarded the study of *appearance* as largely immaterial to that of *reality*.) The thing-quality paradigm is central to Goodman's discussion: "I shall confine myself as far as I can to language that does not imply that there are entities other than individuals [i.e., *things*]" (p. 26). The notions of *thing* and *property* constitute the fundamental elements of Goodman's construction (see pp. 93ff.). Despite some misgivings (p. 302), Goodman exploits and places emphasis on the analogy of time and space (pp. 298–302). Process as such is conspicuously absent from his appearance ontology, though there is some discussion of *change* (pp. 93–99, 300–301). However, he construes change as being simply the replacement of one static quality by another—a change of color is his paradigm (p. 93). In consequence, the discussion of change, instead of leading in the direction of a consideration of processes, reinforces the initial penchant toward the thing-quality doctrine. Throughout his analysis, the approach is such that his book can be counted as a part of the "revolt against process."

The journal literature also affords numerous illustrations of the tendency of thought under consideration. Michael Dummett has written most ingeniously "A Defense of McTaggart's Proof of the Unreality of Time."[4] The existence of a strict analogy between space (or one dimension thereof) and time is cleverly argued in Donald Williams' passionate article "The Myth of Passage,"[5] and his thesis finds enthusiastic support in Richard Taylor's article "Spatial and Temporal Analogies and the Concept of Identity."[6] The ontological fundamentality of things, preeminently physical objects, is taken for granted by authors too numerous to catalogue (although the *grounds* for viewing things as more basic than processes are but seldom canvassed).[7]

The same general tendency is found in D. S. Schwayder's monograph *Modes of Referring and the Problem of Universals: An Essay in Metaphysics.*[8] Schwayder's ontological perspective is completely thing oriented, partly as the result, partly as the cause of his approaching the problem from the standpoint of the theory of reference (i.e., thing reference) in the tradition of Bertrand Russell. The most general designators occurring in Schwayder's discussion are "object" and "existent," both construed as referring to *things,* not processes. The paradigm "thing" is, as usual, a material object, that is, an *inert* thing, agents not being construed qua agents but regarded as material objects. The mathematically inspired approach of this "essay in metaphysics" is such that change, time, and process enter in only the most incidental ways (e.g., pp. 17–18, 22, 32–33, 86–89; where time, duly spatialized, enters generally in connection with the search for "a criterion of identity"—of course, for "objects"). Time, for Schwayder, is essentially a species of "location" (in a somewhat technical sense of this term). All in all, a tendency to downgrade processes—subordinating them to substance where not dismissing them outright—has been pervasive throughout recent Anglo-American philosophy.

3. Strawson's Position

In no recent work does this tendency receive stronger endorsement than in P. F. Strawson's *Individuals: An Essay in Descriptive Metaphysics*.[9] No brief summary can do justice to the subtlety of Strawson's analysis; thus I waive charges of errors of omission in my discussion of his book. But I think that no errors of commission are involved in saying that Strawson urges the following theses, all of which fall squarely within the theater of our "revolt against process":

1. Material bodies are to be taken as the basic paradigm of "objects" in ontological discussion.

2. The concept of a person adds to the concept of a thing (material body)—most significantly the capacities for thought or consciousness, whereas capacities for initiating action are largely irrelevant or perhaps merely unimportant (except in that the capacity for action is a prerequisite for having intentions).

3. Time plays no significantly independent metaphysical role—it can virtually always be what might be called "space hyphenated" in our discussions, as in speaking of a "space-time network" or of "spatiotemporal particulars."

4. The principal metaphysical role of time is thus to serve as part of a "spatiotemporal network" that permits the identification and reidentification of "particulars" (i.e., things, preeminently material bodies).

5. Processes are ontologically subordinate to things.

Strawson's book has the outstanding merit of meeting head-on the question of the claims of process to assuming a place of importance in metaphysics. In section 7 of chapter 1—the longest single section of his book —Strawson labors manfully to show that things are ontologically prior to processes. I shall not enter here into any extensive consideration of Strawson's extremely interesting discussion. It will suffice for present purposes to show that his entire approach to questions of ontological status is based upon an unacceptable premise. The most vulnerable premise here is Strawson's fundamental thesis that identifiability-dependence constitutes the appropriate criterion for ontological priority.[10]

Strawson's entire analysis rests on the supposition that we will succeed in the search for ontological priority once we have seen "whether there is reason to suppose that identification of particulars belonging to some categories is in fact dependent on identification of particulars belonging to others, and whether there is any category of particulars which is basic in this respect" (pp. 40–41). Thus the particulars of category 1 are ontologically more basic than those of category 2 when, in order to identify a (particular) thing belonging to category 2 in order to make a linguistically self-contained (nonostensive) "identifying reference" to a particular of category 2, we must first make an identifying reference to a particular of category 1. This approach to the determination of what is ontologically "basic" on the grounds of linguistic practice alone lies open to serious objections.

First, the approach downplays ontology altogether by staying entirely on the side of epistemic *rationes cognoscendi,* dealing exclusively with the question of how we go about identifying things without any concern for other, for example, nonconceptual, dependence relationships among things. (It is a contemplatable prospect that this epistemological approach is the proper way of "doing" ontology, but this is certainly something to be argued for rather than merely assumed.)

Second, tying questions of what is or is not "ontologically basic" to particular identification procedures is an extremely questionable strategy, even on the surface of it. If (as, in some contexts, we unquestionably do in actual practice) we generally identified persons by means of serial numbers—so that, to make an identifying reference to someone, we would first have to make an identifying reference to a number (namely his or hers)—this identifiability dependence would scarcely entitle anyone to regard persons as ontologically subordinate to numbers.[11] Given, for example, the admitted fact that we identify stars in the nonvisible range in terms of their location with respect to visible stars, does such identifiability dependence establish the visible stars as *ontologically* prior to the nonvisible ones in some genuine sense?

The third and perhaps most serious objection is best put in the form of a question: Why should we use *identifiability* dependence as the criterion for ontological precedence? Consider some alternatives. We might, with equal *prima facie* plausibility, say that the things of category 1 are "ontologically prior" to those of category 2 if

to *describe* a member of category 2, we must mention (or invoke) a member of category 1;

to *account for* (explain the occurrence or existence of) a member of category 2, we must mention (or invoke) a member of category 1;

to *predict* the emergence of a member of category 2, we must . . . ;

to *produce* (make, construct, synthesize, etc.) a member of category 2, we must . . . .

This list could be prolonged, of course, but it is long enough to make our point: Why is *identifiability* dependence to be selected as the touchstone of ontological priority, rather than, say, description-dependence or explanation-dependence or prediction-dependence or production-dependence, and so on? It will clearly not do to argue that identification is *logically* prior to these other resources because they presuppose it. After all we can (for instance) explain certain phenomena without *identifying* anything—that is, on the basis of a classification (or a description) rather than an identification. And in the second place, (particular) identification is patently not a requisite for prediction or production: when I teach you how to bake a carrot cake, there is no question of its antecedent identification, nor need one identify anything when predicting a fall in the stock market.

The point of the foregoing paragraph would be harmless for Strawson's argument only if all the mentioned alternative criteria for "ontological priority" uniformly awarded the palm of victory to things over processes. But just this is what they clearly do not do. One could plausibly argue, for example, that, in the sense of criterion (2), processes are ontologically prior to physical things, since the existence of (given) material objects can be fully accounted for only in terms of the processes that lead to their realization (with the possible exception of creations *ex nihilo*, such as that of hydrogen atoms in some cosmologies).

These considerations (among others) cast substantial doubt on the fitness of identifiability dependence in the sense of Strawson's discussion to provide a suitable means for deciding which of two groups of particulars is ontologically "basic." The collapse of this fundamental criterion would also bring down the entire edifice of argumentation that Strawson builds up to justify the ontological elevation of *things* (material bodies) over processes.[12]

Moreover, even if one were to concede the validity of the epistemological approach to ontology, it might well turn out that things will not win out over processes. After all, our contact with things comes about through direct sensory observation and vicarious data derived from hearing (and reading) the discourse of others. But clearly these modes of acquiring information about things involve what even "our ordinary conceptual scheme" represents as processes—seeing, touching, and so on. Our everyday view of things is surely such that our commerce with things transpires through the mediation of interactive processes—not only physically but also epistemically. Even *identification* is itself a (cognitive) process, and we generally identify existing things by means of *instructions* as to what one is to do to establish contact with the item at issue—"The North Star is the light source you will see when . . . ," and "If you'll just follow along this direction I'm pointing out to you now, then after ten minutes of brisk walking you'll see a large gray building that . . ."

4. Retrospect

While much of recent analytical philosophy confronts us with a "revolt against process," such earlier metaphysicians as Peirce, James, and Whitehead put process at the forefront of their ontological syntheses.[13] Now those given to indulging in psychoanalytical mythopoesis could enjoy themselves a good deal at the expense of the philosophical tendency being called into question. They could take delight in discovering that the preference for things-with-timeless-qualities is merely a latter-day variant of the eternal verities of earlier philosophy and would doubtless discern in the revolt against process a yearning for an abiding haven in a changing world. But this sort of mythopoesis is too facile to be profitable, and too *ad hominem* to be persuasive.

The downgrading of process appears as a natural development in light of the usual dialectic of intellectual history. From this perspective, it is not surprising that the concept of process should suffer at the hand of ontological theorists of the present day. For this would appear to be a predictable reaction against the metaphysicians of an earlier philosophical generation, of whom the most influential tended (like Bergson, James, and Dewey) to give process a place of perhaps exaggerated importance at the very center of the ontological state.

There is, of course, a possibility that the latter-day tendency is right— that somehow in the final analysis the thing-quality paradigm is indeed ontologically fundamental and process not only secondary, subordinate, but perhaps even unimportant. Yet not only is this far from self-evident; it is also *prima facie* quite implausible. The curious and distressing fact is that, with the notable exception of the problematic arguments in Strawson's *Individuals*, one finds that nowhere in the literature of the revolt against process are we given any substantial, explicit, head-on attack upon process, designed to establish the appropriateness of its subordination to the thing-quality paradigm. Surely debatable theses on fundamental issues ought not to be allowed to carry the day by default. If the "revolt against process" is to score a philosophically meaningful victory, the revolutionists will have to gain their ground in pitched battle. However variable and fluctuating processes may be, *process* is too pervasive and persistent to wither away if only the partisans of the thing-and-quality ontology persist in ignoring or disparaging it long enough.[14]

5. On Situating Process Philosophy

How does process philosophy fit into the larger scheme of things? As we enter a new century, it is becoming clear that historians are inclined to picture the present condition of philosophy in terms of a great divide. On the one side here lies so called Analytic philosophy—the tradition evolved in the wake of thinkers like Frege, Moore, Russell, and C. D. Broad. On the other side lies the tradition of Continental philosophy, which evolved in the wake of thinkers like Heidegger, Cassirer, and Gadamer in Germany, and Croce or Sartre elsewhere. The one movement aims at precision and clarity, taking as its model the formal or the empirical sciences; the other aims at historical depth and hermeneutical generality, taking a humanistic and value-oriented approach.

The general tendency among students and historians of philosophy has been to see process philosophy as firmly emplaced on the Continental side. Classical precursors of processism are seen to include figures like Leibniz and Hegel and its later exponents on the American scene comprising such continentally influenced thinkers as Peirce, Whitehead, and Hartshorne. Antiprocessists, however, have been principally recruited from the Analytic side of the divide and include such philosophers as Ramsey, Quine, and Strawson, logically inspired theorists who work under the influence of an essentially static picture of the world drawn from logical theory. In the setting of this perspective, students and devotees of process philosophy alike have viewed this philosophical approach as positioned squarely on the Continental side of the divide.

Such a view is not without its justification. For it must, of course, be recognized and acknowledged that process philosophy poses problems of assessment—of prioritization and doctrinal evaluation—that involve intimate doctrinal as well as historical affinities with Continental thought. Processists are concerned with issues of priority and significance, of interpersonal action and interaction, and of larger human concerns in a way that is generally—and rightly—seen as central in the Continental tradition of philosophizing.

All the same, it has to be said that this is very far from being all that there is to it. To think that process philosophy can simply be integrated into the Continental framework is in error. This error is one of omission rather than commission. The fact is that there is nothing inherently one-sided about process philosophy. On the contrary, it is very much of a broad church—a large-scale project that has affinities and involvements across the entire range of philosophical concerns.

In particular, as the issues with which these present deliberations began clearly indicate, process philosophy is also involved with a whole list of fundamentally analytical issues, such as

How does the concept of processes work?

What is the nature of a process?

How is the conception of a process bound up with that of time?

How is the temporal aspect of processes to be understood?

What is involved with the existence of processes? How are we to understand the claim that a center process actually exists?

What sorts of processes are there? How are processes to be classified, and what is the typology of process?

Questions of this sort are quintessentially analytical in character. And it is no less clear that any process philosophy that can stake a cogent claim to adequacy must come to terms with them. In neglecting such issues, an exposition of the problem would be greatly defective, and on this basis, it becomes clear that process philosophy has an inherently analytical dimension that functions to block the adequacy of any account that one-sidedly positions it on the Continental side of the divide.

Any fair-minded and conscientious view of the matter must acknowledge that process philosophy is a complex and multifaceted project that resists any attempt to constrain it neatly and narrowly in the preestablished philosophical textbook typology. Process philosophy is so many-sided that it abuts on every area of philosophical concern.

This line of thought brings us to another related point. In a classic paper presented in 1908, the then prominent and influential Johns Hopkins University philosopher Arthur O. Lovejoy gave reign to his not inconsiderable annoyance with pragmatism.[15] "What," he asked, "is it that those pesky pragmatists want anyway?" In probing for an answer to this question, Lovejoy provided a discussion, provocatively entitled "The Thirteen Pragmatisms," enumerating so many different pragmatic themes and theories that each of these rather different versions of pragmatism varied from the rest and as often as not actually came into logical conflict with some of them. In scanning this complex and disunified scene, Lovejoy concluded that pragmatism is not a coherent position in philosophy. The doctrine, so he contended, simply self-destructs through inner fission. However, Lovejoy's plausible-looking objection to pragmatism commits a series of far-reaching mistakes. It fails to acknowledge and accommodate the fundamental differences in philosophical teaching between a *philosophical doctrine or position,* on the one hand, and the *philosophical approach or tendency,* on the other. The one is a specific and definite substantive position, the other a generic and potentially diffuse doctrinal tendency. And it is, of course, mistaken to look for doctrinal unanimity within any broad philosophical tendency.

The fact is that any substantial philosophical tendency—realism, idealism, materialism—is a fundamentally prismatic complex , each in a broad programmatic tendency that can be worked out in various directions. In each instance, insisting on having a single, definite, monolithic core doctrinal position would indulge an inappropriate essentialism. Each such tendency is inherently many-sided and multiplex. This, of course, holds not just for pragmatism but for process philosophy as well. It, too, is not a doctrinally monolithic tendency predicated in a particular thesis or theory but a general and programmatic approach. To see it as a unified doctrine would be as erroneous as identifying it with the teachings and ideas of a single thinker.

Like any philosophical movement of larger scale, process philosophy has internal divisions and variations. One important difference at issue here is rooted in the issue of what type of process is taken as paramount and paradigmatic. Some contributors (especially Bergson) see organic processes as central and other sorts of processes as modeled on or superengrafted upon them. Others (especially William James) based their ideas of process on a psychological model and saw human thought as idealistically paradigmatic. Or, turning from substance to methodology, it might be observed that some processists (e.g., Whitehead) articulated their position in terms that are rooted in physics, whereas others (especially Bergson) relied more on biological considerations. There are, of course, sociocultural processists like John Dewey. Such differences not withstanding, there are family-resemblance commonalties of theme and emphasis that leave the teachings of process theorists in the position of variations on a common approach. So in the end it is, or should be, clear that the unity of process philosophy is not doctrinal but thematic; it is not a consensus or a thesis but rather a mere diffuse matter of type and approach. All this is something to which a Lovejoy-style complaint about doctrinal diversity would do serious injustice.

The satisfactory articulation of any sort of process philosophy requires the sort of evaluative appraisal and historical contextualization that characterizes Continental philosophy. It also requires the sort of conceptual clarification and explanatory systematization that characterize Analytic philosophy. The long and short of it is that process philosophy covers too vast a range to belong to one side or the other of this continental divide of twentieth century philosophy: its scope and range of concern are too big for it to be owned as an exclusive possession of any one particular philosophical approach or tendency. There is good reason for accepting this state of things as only fitting and proper, for in this respect process philosophy is simply being true to itself. Process thought, after all, inclines toward viewing reality as a complex manifold of varied but interrelated processes. And just exactly this is true, to all appearances, of process philosophy itself.

6. Process Philosophy and Pragmatism

Process philosophy and pragmatism represent two areas of America's most substantial and distinctive contributions to philosophy. It is of interest to take note of their inherent conceptual interrelationship. The core idea of pragmatism is that the natural and appropriate way to assess the adequacy of any teleologically goal-directed practice is through its effectiveness and efficiency in realizing the objectives at issue. The core idea of process philosophy is a dynamism that prioritizes processes for things—an ontological view that does not look to things but to processes governed by laws of operation that themselves are not necessarily stable but potentially changeable and evolving. Let us consider how these positions are interrelated, beginning with the limits of process to pragmatism.

From our standpoint, an intelligent being is the most significant, and *xyz* processes are those managed by agents with a view to the realization of some objective. It is clear that pragmatism must reign supreme in this domain because the natural and evident way to assess the adequacy of such a teleologically goal-directed mode of operation will point to the question of the efficacy and efficiency with which it facilitates realization of the goal at issue.

Increasingly, the limits of pragmatism to process are also clear. Pragmatism is concerned with teleologically efficient agency, and purposive agency is always a matter of procedure and process. In its concern for agency, pragmatism looks inevitably to procedural processes. Moreover, these processes themselves are caught in a procedural web. They, too—our mode of operation—are themselves always evolving in the direction of greater efficiency and are thus geared to a cause of processual development.

In sum, pragmatism and process philosophy are interrelated by a common instrument in concern for operational efficacy in the course of processual development. Accordingly, pragmatists and processists alike prioritize a concern for effectiveness and efficiency in the context of teleological processes. In the final analysis each of these two schools is deeply committed to heeding the issues and ideas that are pivotal for the position of the other. There is no question that these two doctrinal positions stand in fruitful symbiosis.

CHAPTER FOUR

Human Agency as Process

1. The Problem of Act Description

Human action, unprominent process though it may be in the grand scheme of things, is bound to be a topic of particular interest and concern to us humans. In addressing the issues that arise here we confront such fundamental questions as

What is the nature of action?

What is an action?

What sorts of things are actions?

The present discussion will approach the key question of *What is an action?* obliquely, from the angle of the question *How are actions to be described?* It proceeds in the expectation that by shedding light upon the descriptive characterization of action it will prove possible to throw some informative light upon the nature of action itself.[1]

2. Some Fundamental Contrasts

Actions are agent-managed processes. In delineating the class of phenomena at issue here, the following fundamental contrasts are instructive.

Actions versus impersonal processes. An action will always be something done by an agent. The locution "he/she/it (the agent) did *X*" must always be applicable if an action is to be at issue. This convention differentiates *actions* (e.g., Smith's stirring the cup) from the *impersonal processes* of inert nature (e.g., the evaporation of the spilled drops).

Actions versus passions. In saying something is an instance of an agent's action, we insist on its being a part of the agent's actual active endeavor. This sets his actions apart from those things that merely "happen to" him—for example, his *sitting down* (because he feels weak) from his *falling down* (because he slipped on a banana peel). But many sorts of things other than their actions can also be said to be done by agents. The remaining distinctions will exhibit some of these.

Action versus mere behavior. An agent can be said to "do" various things (gasp or hiccup, tremble with fear or beam with joy) with respect to which the exercise of agency does not come into play. Such doings are not to be classed as actions: an action—in contrast with something that "happens to" one or that one "just happens to do"—is an item of behavior over whose occurrence one exercises *control*. The element of aim/objective/intent is ever present with actions, even where they are habitual or automatic.

Actions versus achievements. The distinction between activity verbs (e.g., listening for, looking at, searching for) and achievement verbs (hearing, seeing, finding) is familiar from other contexts. The former category will represent actions, but the latter—in which only the result of the activity is at issue—will not. The king's going through the crowning ceremony is an action, but his succeeding to the throne is not.

Refraining versus nonaction. Inaction has two distinctly different modes. The one is refraining: When sitting at my desk writing I may refrain from scratching an itching mosquito bite—that is, I "hold myself back" or "keep myself from" doing a certain action. This sort of restraining oneself from doing something that is at issue in refraining is importantly different from a second type of inaction. For example, when sitting at my desk writing, there is an endless number of things I am not doing: reading the newspaper, chatting with a friend, driving a car, and so on. These *nonactions* are not doings of any sort; I am not somehow active in keeping myself from doing them. Thus, unlike re-fraining, they are not actions at all. There is a critical difference be-tween doing not-*X*, which is an action, and not-doing *X*, which need not be.

Actions versus mental acts. An action must have the aspect of physical activity, either positively by way of doing or negatively by way of refrain-ing. Actions involve physical processes. Thus purely mental acts done solely *in foro interno* cannot qualify as actions. Working out a sum on paper involves actions; working it out in one's head does not. Giving overt verbal agreement is an action; giving tacit assent is not. Being worried is not in itself an action, though pacing worriedly is. Every ac-tion must have an overt physical component and involves bodily activ-ity of some sort. It is thus no accident that paradigm actions are done by *persons*—that is, agents with corporeal bodies.

So much for the preliminary delineation of the sphere of "actions." We shall now turn to our main task: an examination of the descriptive aspects of action.

3. Descriptive Aspects of Action

The conceptual tools for what might be called the *canonical description* of an action deserve special attention. The object here is to give a com-prehensive *inventory of the key generic elements of actions,* so as to pro-vide a classificatory matrix of rubrics under which the essential fea-tures of actions can be classed. The following tabulation represents an attempt to compile such an inventory:

1. Agent (*who* did it?)
2. Act-type (*what* did he do?)[2]
3. Modality of action (*how* did he do it?)
   a. Modality of manner (*in what way* did he do it?)
   b. Modality of means (*by what means* did he do it?)
4. Setting of action (*in what context* did he do it?)

   a. Temporal aspect (*when* did he do it? *how long* did it take?)[3]
   b. Spatial aspect (*where* did he do it?)
   c. Circumstantial aspect (*under what circumstances* did he do it?)
5. Rationale of action (*why* did he do it?)
   a. Causality (*what caused* him to do it?)
   b. Finality (*with what aim* did he do it?)
   c. Intentionality (*from what motives* did he do it?)[4]

The Agent

The agent of an action may be an individual or a group that is capable of action (e.g., crowds, boards of directors, and parliaments). Groups can act distributively, as single individuals (as when the audience applauds), or collectively as a corporate whole (as when Congress votes to override a presidential veto).

The Act-Type

An act-type can be specified at varying levels of concreteness. It can be a *merely* generic act-type (e.g., "the opening of a window" and "the sharpening of a pencil"). Such a generic act-type characterization can be rendered more specific ("the opening of *this* window" and "the sharpening of *that* pencil") whenever a concrete object involved in the action is indicated (this window, that pencil). Such a *specific act-type* is one that, though of a general type, involves a concrete particular. Obviously, any particular action can be described (i.e., placed within descriptive types) at varying levels of generality. In a particular case we might say "He raised *a* hand" or "He raised *his right* hand."

The Modality of Action

Modality concerns the ways and means of the thing. Consider an action to be done—for example, that Jones shook hands with Smith. Did he do it firmly or weakly, rapidly or slowly, clumsily or deftly, gently or roughly? All of these endlessly variant characterizations of the way in which the action was accomplished are part of the modality of action.

Some action qualifications seem on first view to indicate the agent's state of mind but are actually descriptive of his manner of acting. Thus "he sighed contentedly" or "he said good-bye sadly" describe the manner of his sigh or farewell.

"White opened the curtains." Did he do so with the pull-rope, or with his hands, or with a stick? Such characterizations of the means (instruments) by which the action was done relate to the modality of means. The means can be generic ("He killed the man with *a* revolver") or specific ("He killed the man with *this* .35 caliber, Smith and Wesson, series 1935c, serial no. 1056773 revolver"). Of course, if Robinson breathed or twiddled his thumbs, it makes little sense to ask about the means by which he did so (though we could, of course, inquire about the manner). Normal bodily movements are accomplished without overt means. Many other types of actions are such that, barring exotic cases, the means of action are implicitly specified within the action-type itself.

The Setting of Action

Consider an act of a certain type to be performed by a certain agent in a certain manner with a certain means ("He opened the can of soup smoothly with a can opener"). The question still remains as to the specific setting of the action that fixes its position in time, and space, and in the course of events (his doing so in the kitchen yesterday afternoon while the radio was playing). Every action must have a chronological occasion in occurring at a certain time or times, a positional location in occurring at a certain place or places, and a circumstantial content among other things going on within its relevant environment. The ensemble of these three elements constitutes what we have termed the *setting* of the action.

The Rationale of Action

Consider an action such as Smith's pounding his fist on the table. An explanation of this fact may well proceed in causal terms: he acted "out of rage," or "out of drunkenness," or "by an irrepressible urge," or even "due to posthypnotic suggestion." Such act characterizations represent answers (i.e., partial answers) to the question *Why did he do it?* and they all answer this question in the mode of *causality*. Sometimes this is all there is to it—what the agent does "inadvertently" or "by accident" remains outside the range of motives. It is only countering that such acts of doings numbered among a person's *actions*. Bypassing or, in effect, declaring irrelevant the entire issue of Smith's wishes and desires, such act explanations proceed not in terms of the agent's choices but through the impersonal "forces" that are at work. Denying, or ignoring, that the act was a matter of the agent's reason, they address themselves to the purely *causal* aspect of the question of what led him to do it.[5]

When an agent's action was a matter of choice—that is, was something he "chose" rather than something he "was caused" to do—the aspect of finality comes upon the scene, and we can ask "*With what aim did he do it?*" Although causes also provide answers to the question "What led him to do it?", motive and reasons alone answer the question "What *considerations* led him to do it? (Both causal and motivational explanations can in many cases be given of one and the same action—e.g., Smith's sitting down when he feels his knees giving way because of dizziness.) One can, accordingly, inquire into the agent's purposes, wishes, goals, and objectives: his reasons, objectives, and intentions, saying such things as that he did it "out of ambition," or "out of concern for her feelings," or "out of avarice" (i.e., for reasons of prestige, advancement, gain, and so on). When an act was a matter of the agent's volition, such characterizations tell us what objectives were operative in his doing it; they related to the finalistic aspect of the action.

Consider the following group of contrasts: voluntarily/involuntarily, deliberately/inadvertently (or accidentally), intentionally/unintentionally (or by mistake), consciously/out of habit (or automatically), knowingly/unwittingly (or unthinkingly), willingly/unwillingly (or reluctantly).[6] All these relate to what may in the aggregate be called the explanatory aspect of action and set a general frame of reference within which the specific issue of causal versus motivational explanations can be posed. Clearly, if *X* did *A* unwittingly and involuntarily, out of habit, an explanation along causal lines is called for, whereas if *X* did it consciously and deliberately we would require a motivational explanation.[7] What someone does would not even qualify as an actual action if it were not the sort of thing standardly done for motives or out of motivated but automatized habits. In full-fledged action—unlike mere behavior—the motivational aspect must always play a role, since some element of volition will always be present here.

The *rationale* of action, on the one hand, and its *type-modality-setting,* on the other, reflect the dichotomous nature of the concept of action. Like the concept of a *person* in general, in which physical and mental aspects are inseparably united, the concept of action has both *overt,* physical and observable, and *covert,* mental and unobservable, involvements. The overt side relates to the issue of *what* he did and its ramifications into *how and in what context* he did it. The covert side relates to certain considerations about his *state of thought* (thoughts, intentions, motives, awareness, and so on) relating to the action. This latter aspect of action is comprehended under our rubric of the *rationale* of action.

It might be said that one ought to separate these issues of explicability from the other perhaps more strictly descriptive aspects of the characterization of an action. "Keep," so the advice might run, "*what* the agent did sharply apart from the issue of *why* he did it." But this is simply not feasible. Action is an inherently two-sided process, and the language of human action is everywhere permeated by the coloration of intentionality and purposiveness. Even in such simple locutions as "He gave her the book," "He turned on the light," or "He brandished his cane," we find not simply behavioristically overt descriptions of matter in motion but implicit suggestions as to the intentional aspects of the transaction ("gave" versus "handed," "turned on" versus "caused to go on," "brandished" versus "moved").

However, maintaining a line of separation between the *description* of an action and its *evaluation* is feasible in principle and desirable in practice. Unlike saying "he did it slowly," saying "he did it wisely" has no bearing on *how* he did it. There are a vast host of act-characterizing terms bearing upon the evaluative assessment of actions: Was the act prudent or rash, considerate or thoughtless, courteous or rude, appropriate or inappropriate? Such issues relate to the "external" evaluation of the action, not to its actual "internal" depiction. They are thus not a proper part of our survey of the descriptive elements of an action.

Again, certain act characterizations depict not so much the action itself as the relationship it bears to other actions of the agent himself or of people in general. Was the act typical or atypical, characteristic or unusual, expected or unexpected? Such considerations, though descriptive rather than evaluative in nature, have their primary orientation directed away from the action itself. Something similar obtains with respect to adverbs that describe not an action itself but its antecedents or results. If *X* did *A* "for the first time in history" or "in vain" or "prematurely," these qualifiers do not describe the action; instead they indicate its relationships to extraneous occurrences. Here, too, we shift the focus of consideration away from the internalities of the action itself.[8]

4. The Problem of Infinite Divisibility

The common-language distinction between individual actions (e.g., the turning of a key in a lock) and complex courses of action (e.g., the successive placement of the dial of a combination lock into a sequential series of appropriate settings) is well known. But is this distinction viable? Is not every action actually a course of actions? Cannot all actions be divided into further components so that there are no ultimate "atomic" actions? To write the word *and,* must we not first write the letter *a,* and in so doing, are we not processing part by part? Not really!

The situation with action is *not* one of endless stages—just as in the racetrack paradox of Zeno of Elea. In "moving his right foot forward one step" Smith does not actually first "move his right foot forward one-half step" and in doing this first "move his right foot forward one-quarter step," ad infinitum. Moving one's foot forward half a step, and so on,[9] are all *potential* actions: they are indeed things one *could* do if the doing of them were "on one's mind" and one *wanted* to do them. But actions are done either intentionally or by habit resulting from intentional actions. In learning to walk we learn to *take steps*—not first to *take quarter steps* and then expand them into half steps and then into full steps. Thus the man who "takes a step forward" in the sorts of circumstances in which the locution would ordinarily be applicable does not perform composite action at all. When one lifts a spoonful of sugar out of the sugar bowl, one does in fact lift out its component grains; but the *action* of taking the sugar is not composed of the *action* of taking the grains. As emphasized earlier, action has an intentional aspect: if it is the spoonful that is "on my mind" (consciously or implicitly) and not at all the grains, then my action in taking the spoonful cannot be subdivided into further actions specified with reference to the grains. Precisely because of the mentalistic finitude of human beings who cannot explicitly entertain an infinity of diverse items in their thought, every compound course of action will be divisible into some terminating, and so finite, list of component simple actions.

5. The Problem of Infinite Polyadicity

In Anthony Kenny's book *Action, Emotion, and Will,* Kenny poses the issue of what he calls the "variable polyadicity" of action.[10] The issue arises from the thesis that any action-performance statement is incomplete and capable of further elaboration. Given that someone "buttered a slice of toast at 3 P.M. yesterday" we can go on to elaborate this endlessly, by specifying more and more detail as to when, where, how, and so on. Kenny thus suggests that any characterization of an action is *inherently incomplete* and capable of fuller and fuller elaboration. "If we cast our net widely enough, we can make 'Brutus killed Caesar' into a sentence which describes, with a certain lack of specification, the whole history of the world."[11] On this view of the matter, every action-presenting statement inevitably is fundamentally incomplete in omitting features essential to the full characterization of the action under discussion (though it may well be fully adequate to all the purposes at issue).

To begin with, this limitless polyadicity does not pertain in any specifically characteristic way to actions as such but rather to *descriptions* in general. In describing anything, we can always provide endlessly greater detail about its specific features and its relations to other things. Completeness in description is never possible. This inherent incompleteness of descriptions in general will also pertain to the descriptions of actions in particular. But this circumstance does not betoken any inevitable incompleteness specific to act characterization as such. Nor does it militate against the principal finding of our present discussion, that action descriptions can be analyzed into specifications at varying levels of detail of answers to a manageably small number of questions about different aspects of action. The fact is that although the description of an action can indeed be elaborated more and more (perhaps indefinitely so), this elaboration can be viewed as the increasingly detailed specification of a limited and manageable number of distinctive characteristic aspects of action. Indeed, actions appear to have only a rather modest number of basic *dimensions,* representing the diverse avenues along which the various fundamental aspects of action can be explored in never-ending detail.

The theme of action is a crucial reminder that the realm of process has two sectors: the impersonal and the agent managed. Agents, of course, are only a small factor in nature's scheme of things. And human agents are even more minor. Yet though human actions may be small stuff on the world's large stage of processes, nevertheless they are bound to be of the greatest interest *for us*. And their internal complexity is virtually endless. In particular, creating fictions is a characteristic mode of human agency, and though fact may be stranger than fiction, nevertheless fiction can find material no less vast than that of discernible fact itself. This endless amplifiability of its scope also contributes to the interest of human action as a particularly salient mode of process.[12]

CHAPTER FIVE

Cognitive Processes and Scientific Progress

1. Question Exfoliation

Human knowledge should be thought of as a process rather than merely a product. It is clearly not stable; because ongoing inquiry leads to new and often dissonant findings and discoveries, knowledge emerges in phases and stages through processes that engender an ever-changing state-of-the-art. The coordination between questions and bodies of knowledge means that in the course of cognitive progress the state of questioning changes no less drastically than the state of knowledge. Cognitive change regarding answers inevitably carries in its wake erotetic change with respect to questions, since alterations in the membership of our body of knowledge will afford new presuppositions for further questions that were not available before.

The course of erotetic in relation to questions change is no less dramatic than that of cognitive change in relation to knowledge. *A change of mind* about the appropriate answer to some question will unravel the entire fabric of questions that presupposed this earlier answer. If we change our mind regarding the correct answer to one member of a chain of questions, then the whole of a subsequent course of questioning may well collapse. If we abandon the luminiferous ether as a vehicle for electromagnetic radiation, then we lose at one stroke the whole host of questions about its composition, structure, mode of operation, origin, and so on.

Epistemic change over time thus relates not only to what is *known* but also to what can be *asked*. The accession of "new knowledge" opens up new questions. And when the epistemic status of a presupposition changes from acceptance to abandonment or rejection, we witness the disappearance of various old ones through dissolution. Questions regarding the modus operandi of phlogiston, the behavior of caloric fluid, and the character of faster-than-light transmissions are all questions that have become lost to modern science because they involve presuppositions that have been abandoned. The question solved in one era could well not even have been posed in another. The British philosopher of science W. Stanley Jevons put it well over a century ago: "Since the time of Newton and Leibniz realms of problems have been solved which before were hardly conceived as matters of inquiry. . . . May we not repeat the words of Seneca . . . *Veniet tempus, quo posteri nostri tam aperta nos nescisse mirentur* [A time will come when our posterity will marvel that such obvious things were unknown to us]."[1]

Questions cluster together in groupings that constitute a line of inquiry. They stand arranged in duly organized and sequential families, the answering of a given question yielding the presuppositions for yet further questions that would not have arisen had the former questions not been answered. (Think here of the game of twenty questions—not until after we establish that a species of dog is at issue does it become appropriate to ask whether a large or small sort of dog is involved.)

Inquiry is a dialectical process, a step-by-step exchange of query and response that produces sequences within which the answers to our questions ordinarily open up yet further questions. This leads to a cyclic process with the following structure:

[Presupposition]——▶ [Question]——▶ [Answer]——▶ [Implication thereof]

Such a cycle—an "erotetic cycle"—determines a *course of inquiry* that is set by an initial, controlling question together with the ancillary questions to which it gives rise and whose solutions are seen as facilitating its resolution. One question *emerges* from another in such a course of inquiry whenever it is only after we have answered the latter that the former becomes posable. There is accordingly a natural stratification in the development of questions. A question cannot arise before its time has come: certain questions cannot even be posed until others have already been resolved, because the resolution of these others is presupposed in their articulations. The unfolding of such a series provides a direction of search—of research—in question-answering inquiry. It gives the business of knowledge a developmental cast, shifting matters from a static situation to a dynamical one.

The conception of a course of inquiry has important ramifications. For one thing, it indicates graphically how, as our cognitive efforts proceed, our questions often come to rest on an increasingly cumbersome basis, with the piling up of an increasingly detailed and content-laden family of available presuppositions. Moreover, it serves to clarify how *a change of mind* regarding the appropriate answer to some earlier question then the whole of the subsequent questioning process may collapse as its presuppositions become untenable, rendering the course of erotetic change no less dramatic than that of cognitive change regarding matters of accepted knowledge.

Cognitive progress is commonly thought of in terms of the discovery of new facts—new information about things. But the situation is actually more complicated, because not only *knowledge* but also *questions* must come into consideration. Progress on the side of *questions* is also a mode of cognitive progress, correlative with—and every bit as important as—progress on the side of *information*. The questions opened up for our consideration are as much a characteristic of a "state of knowledge" as are the theses that it endorses.

2. Kant's Principle

New knowledge that emerges from the progress of knowledge can bear very differently on the matter of questions. Specifically, we can discover

1. new (that is, *different*) answers to old questions;
2. new questions;
3. the inappropriateness or illegitimacy of our old questions.

With (1) we learn that the wrong answer has been given to an old question, thereby uncovering an error of commission in our previous questioning-answering endeavors. With (2) we discover that questions have not heretofore been posed at all, thereby uncovering an error of omission in our former questioning-asking endeavors. Finally, with (3) we find that we have asked the wrong question altogether, thereby uncovering an error of commission in our former questioning-asking endeavors, which are now seen to rest on incorrect presuppositions (and are thus generally bound up with type (1) discoveries). Three rather different sorts of cognitive progress are thus involved here—different from one another and from the traditional view of cognitive progress in terms of a straightforward "accretion of further knowledge."

The coming to be and passing away of questions is a phenomenon that can be mooted on this basis. A question *arises* at time *t* if it then can meaningfully be posed because all its presuppositions are then accepted as true. A question *dissolves* at time *t* if one or another of its previously accepted presuppositions is no longer accepted. Any state of science will remove certain questions from the agenda and dismiss them as inappropriate. Newtonian dynamics dismissed the question "What cause is operative to keep a body in movement (with a uniform velocity in a straight line) once an impressed force has set it into motion?" Modern quantum theory does not allow us to ask "What caused this atom on californium to disintegrate after exactly 32.53 days, rather than, say, a day or two later?" Scientific questions should thus be regarded as occurring in a *historical* setting. They arise at some juncture and not at others; they can be born and then die away.

This leads to the theme of fallibilism once more. A body of knowledge may well answer a question only provisionally, in a tone of voice so tentative or indecisive as to indicate that further information is actually needed to enable us to settle the matter with confidence. But even if it does firmly and unequivocally support a certain resolution, this circumstance can never be viewed as absolutely final. What is seen as the correct answer to a question at one stage of the cognitive venture, may, of course, cease to be so regarded at another, later stage.[2] Given the answer that a particular state of science S sees as appropriate to a question Q, we can never preclude the prospect that some superior successor to S will eventually emerge and that it will then transpire that some different answer is in order—one that is actually *inconsistent* with the earlier one.

The second of the three modes of erotetic discovery is particularly significant. The phenomenon of the ever-continuing "birth" of new questions was first emphasized by Immanuel Kant, who saw the development of natural science in terms of a continually evolving cycle of questions and answers, where, *"every answer given on principles of experience begets a fresh question, which likewise requires its answer* and thereby clearly shows the insufficiency of all scientific modes of explanation to satisfy reason."[3] This claim suggests the following principle of question propagation—Kant's principle, as we shall call it: *The answering of our factual (scientific) questions always paves the way to further as yet unanswered questions.* Note, however, that Kant's principle can be construed in two rather different ways:

1. A *universalized* mode: *Each* specific (particular) question Q that can be raised on the basis of a state-of-knowledge S engenders a (Q-correlative) line of questioning that leads ultimately to a question Q' whose answer lies outside of S—a question that

forces an eventual shift from S to some suitably augmented or revised modification thereof.

2. A *particular* mode that arises when the italicized *each* of the preceding formula is replaced by *some*.

On the first construction, science is an essentially divergent process, with questions leading to more questions in such a way that the erotetic agenda of successive stages of science is ever increasing in scope and size. This view was endorsed by Jevons, who wrote, "As it appears to me, the supply of new and unexplained facts is divergent in extent, so that the more we have explained, the more there is to explain."[4] However, the second construction is a far more modest proposition, which merely sees science as self-perpetuating with some new questions arising at every stage, thereby opening up a window of opportunity for the investigation of new issues. On this basis, the question agenda of science is not necessarily a growing one, since questions may well die off by dissolution at a rate roughly equal to that of the birth of new questions.

Kant himself intended the principle in the first (universalized) sense, but it would actually seem more plausible and realistic to adopt it in the second, more modest (particularized) sense. This yields a thesis amply supported by historical experience: that every state-of-the-art condition of questioning ultimately yields, somewhere along the road, a line of questioning that engenders the transition. The states of science are unstable: the natural course of inquiry provides an impetus by which a given state is ultimately led to give way to its successor.

How can this principle possibly be established? What is at issue here is not, of course, simply the merely logico-conceptual point that whenever we introduce a new claim p into the family of what we accept, we can inquire into such matters as the reasons for p's being the case and the relationship of p to other facts that we accept. Rather, the issue pivots on the more interesting fact that new answers generally change the range of presuppositions available for new questions. As we deepen our understanding of the world, new problem areas and new issues are bound to come to the fore. Once we have discovered, for example, that atoms are not really "atomic" but actually have an internal composition and complexity of structure, then questions about this whole "subatomic" domain become available for investigation. At bottom, Kant's principle rests on the insight that no matter what answers are in hand, we can proceed to dig deeper into the how of things by raising yet further questions about the matters involved in these answers themselves. When physicists postulate a new phenomenon, they naturally want to know its character and modus operandi. When chemists synthesize a new substance, they naturally want to know how it interacts with the old ones.

Accordingly, the moving force of inquiry is the existence of questions that are posable relative to the "body of knowledge" of the day but not answerable within it. Inquiry sets afoot a process of a cyclic form depicted in Fig. 5.1. Here the body of "scientific knowledge" S and the cor-

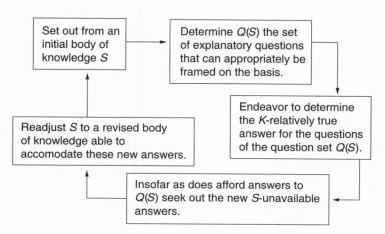

Figure 5.1 The erotetic dynamic of inquiry

relative body of scientific questions $Q(S)$ undergo continual alteration. This process gives rise to successive "stages of knowledge" (with increasing t) together with their associated state-of-the-art stages with regard to questions, $Q(S_t)$. From a statically conceived "body of (scientific) knowledge,"K or S, we are led to a temporalized K_t or S_t, indicative of the inherently dynamical nature of inquiry.

3. Assessing Progress

Various accounts have been proposed to characterize scientific progress in terms of historical tendencies regarding question-and-answer relationships. Perhaps the most rudimentary theory of this sort is the traditional expansionist view that later, more advanced stages of science are characterized as such because they *answer additional questions*—questions over and above those answered at earlier stages of the game:

$$t_1 < t_2 \supset [Q^*(S_{t1}) \subset Q^*(S_{t2})].$$

Here $Q^*(S_t)$ is the set of all S_t-answered questions, including all of those S_t-posable questions for which S_t also provides an answer. This expansionist theory holds that later, superior science answers all of the formerly answered questions (albeit perhaps differently) and, furthermore, answers some previously unanswered questions. Progress, according to this theory, is a matter of knowledge accumulation: as science progresses, the set of answered questions is an ever-growing whole.

Along this line, Popper has suggested that if the "content" of a theory T is construed as the set of all *questions* to which it can provide answers, then a scientific theory might be compared unfavorably with that of its superior successors—their substantive incompatibility notwithstanding—because of proper inclusion with respect to this erotetic mode of "content."[5] On this view, even though T_1 is assertorically incompatible with T_2, we might still be in a position to compare the question sets $Q^*(T_1)$ and $Q^*(T_2)$, and, in particular, might have the inclusion relation that $Q^*(T_1) \subset (Q^*(T_2)$.

But this is nonsense. For let p be a proposition that brings this incompatibility to view, so that T_1 asserts p and T_2 asserts not-p. Then "Why is p the case?" is a question that the theory T_1 not only allows to arise but also presumably furnishes with an answer. So this question belongs to $Q^*(T_1)$. But it cannot belong to $Q^*(T_2)$, because T_2 (ex hypothesi) *violates the question's evident presupposition that* p *is the case.*[6]

If one body of assertions includes the thesis p among its entailments while another fails to include p, then we can always (as earlier) ask the rationale-demanding question "Why is it that p is the case?" with respect to the former, where the presupposition that p is the case is met, but not with respect to the latter, where this presupposition fails. Discordant bodies of (putative) knowledge engender distinct, mutually divergent bodies of questions because they provide the material for distinct sets of background presuppositions. Modern medicine no longer asks about the operations of Galenic humors; present-day physics no longer asks about the structure of the luminiferous ether. Future physics may well no longer ask about the characteristics of quarks. When science abandons certain theoretical entities, it also foregoes (gladly) the opportunity to ask questions about them.

In the actual course of scientific progress, we see not only *gains* in question resolution but also *losses*. Aristotle's theory of natural place provided an explanation for the "gravitational attraction" of the earth in a way that Newton's theory did not. Descartes' vortex theory could answer the question of why all the planets revolve about the sun in the same direction—a question for which Newton's celestial mechanics had no answer. The earlier chemistry of affinities could explain why certain chemical interactions take place and others do not, a phenomenon for which Dalton's quantitative theory had no explanation. The theory of progress through an ongoing enlargement in point of question resolution is patently untenable.

A second theory of progress takes the rather different approach of associating scientific progress with an expansion in our question horizon. It holds that later, superior science will always enable us to *pose additional questions:*

$$t_1 < t_2 \supset [Q(S_{t1}) \subset Q(S_{t2})].$$

Scientific progress is now seen as a process of enlarging the question agenda by uncovering new questions. More questions rather than more answers are seen as the key: progress is a matter of question-cumulativity, with more advanced science making it possible to pose issues that could not be envisaged earlier on.

However, this second approach to progressiveness is also untenable. For just as progress sometimes involves abandoning old answers, it also often involves rejecting old questions. Paul Feyerabend has argued this point cogently.[7] New theories, he holds, generally do not subsume the substantive issues of older ones but instead move off in altogether different directions. At first, the old theory may even be more comprehensive—having had more time for its development. Only gradually does this change. But by then "the slowly emerging conceptive apparatus of the [new] theory soon starts defining its own problems, and earlier problems, facts, and observations are either forgotten or pushed aside as irrelevant." This phenomenon of problem loss invalidates the theory of scientific progress as question cumulation.

A third theory sees scientific progress in terms of an increase in the volume of resolved questions. Thus, Larry Laudan has argued against Popper that scientific progress is not to be understood as arising because the later, superior theories that replace our earlier ones answer all the questions answered by their rival (or earlier) counterparts, plus some additional questions, but rather because the replacing theories answer *more* questions (although not necessarily all of the same questions answered previously).[8] On such a doctrine, progress turns on *a*

numerical increase in the sheer quantity of answered questions; that is, it is
a matter of simply *answering more questions:*

$$t_1 < t_2 \supset [Q^*(S_{t1}) < \# Q^*(S_{t2})].$$

(Here the operation # applied to a set represents a measure of its membership.) But this position also encounters grave difficulties. For how
are we going to do our bookkeeping here? How can we individuate
questions for the counting process? Just how many questions does
"What causes cancer?" amount to? And how can we avoid the ambi-
guity inherent in the fact that once an answer is given, we can always
raise further questions about its inner details and its outer relationships?

Moreover, this position is unpromising as long as we leave the *adequacy* of the answers out of account. In its earliest, animistic stage, for
example, science had answers for everything. Why does the wind blow?
The spirit of the winds arranges it. Why do the tides ebb and flow? The
spirit of the seas sees to it. And so on. Or again take astrology. Why did
X win the lottery and Y get killed in an accident? The conjunction of the
stars provides all the answers. Some of the biggest advances in science
come about when we *reopen* questions—when our answers get unstuck
en masse with the discovery that we have been on the wrong track, that
we do not actually understand something we thought we understood
perfectly well and need new answers to old questions.

A fourth theory sees scientific progress in terms of *a decrease in the
sheer number of unanswered questions,* that is, of *answering fewer questions:*

$$t_1 < t_2 \supset \left[\frac{\# Q^*(S_{t1})}{\# Q(S_{t1})} < \frac{\# Q^*(S_{t2})}{\# Q(S_{t2})} \right].$$

This approach views progress as a matter of agenda diminution. Progressiveness turns on a numerical decrease in the register of unan-

swered questions. But the same line of objection put forth against its predecessor will also tell against this present conception of progress. New discoveries can all too easily raise more questions than we had before. To be sure, the size of this gap between Q and Q^* is something significant—a measure of the size of the second agenda of a given state of the cognitive art. The striving to close this gap by reducing the agenda is a prime mover of scientific inquiry. But it is emphatically not an index of progress.

An increase in the volume of *unanswered* questions is compatible with a more than compensating increase in the volume of *answered* questions. A fifth cognate theory of scientific progress uses the *ratio* of answered to unanswered questions as a touchstone and accordingly sees progressiveness in terms of a *decrease in the relative proportion of answered questions:*

$$t_1 < t_2 \supset \left[\frac{\#Q^*(S_{t1})}{\#Q(S_{t1})} < \frac{\#Q^*(S_{t2})}{\#Q(S_{t2})} \right].$$

But just why should one consider this relationship to be essential to progress? It is perfectly possible, in theory, that scientific progress might be divergent, that particular increases in question-resolving capability might be more than offset by expanding problem horizons. (Ten percent of 10^7 questions is still a substantially bigger proportion than 20 percent of 10^6 questions.) In such circumstances, we could make striking "progress" by way of substantial increases in question-resolving capacity while nevertheless having a smaller *proportion* of answered questions because of the larger volume of new questions. Then, too, questions are not created equal. Clearly, one question can *include* another, as "What causes lightning?" includes "What causes ball lightning?" In the course of answering the one, we are called on to provide an answer for the other. Such relations of inclusion and dominance provide a basis for comparing the "scope" of questions (in one sense of this term) in certain cases—though certainly not in general. They do not enable us to compare the scope of "What causes lightning?" and "What causes tides?" (And even if we could—*per impossible*—measure and compare the "size" of questions in this content-volume-oriented sense, this would afford no secure guide to their relative importance.)

Other approaches to progress are also possible. Some theoreticians have favored yet another, sixth theory—one that sees scientific progress as essentially *ignorance-enlarging*. That is, they regard scientific progress as a matter of *increasing the relative proportion of unanswered questions,* thus simply reversing the inequality of the preceding formula. Along these lines, Jevons wrote, "In whatever direction we extend our investigations and successfully harmonise a few facts, the result is only to raise up a host of other unexplained facts. Can any scientific man venture to state that there is less opening now for new discoveries than there was three centuries ago? Is it not rather true that we have but to open a scientific book and read a page or two, and we shall come to some recorded phenomenon of which no explanation can yet be given? In every such fact there is a possible opening for new discoveries."[9] This theory sees scientific progress as a cognitively divergent process, subject to the condition that the more we know, the more we are brought to the realization of our relative ignorance. But this position also has a serious flaw. For it totally fails to do justice to those—by no means infrequent—stages of the history of science when progress does go along in the manner of the classical pattern of an increase in both the volume and the proportion of resolved questions.

Yet further variant theories along analogous lines see progress as lying in increasing the proportion of answered questions or in decreasing the proportion of unanswered questions (i.e., ignorance reduction), respectively. For reasons closely akin to those already considered, these theories also have vitiating disabilities.

In sum, none of these approaches to progress through question-agenda comparisons offer much promise. The process of scientific inquiry is such that its progress will have to be characterized in altogether different terms of reference. In relating the questions sets $Q(S_t)$ and/or $Q^*(S_t)$ at different times in the manner of the progress theories we have been considering, one operates merely in the realm of appearances—how far the (putative) science of the day can go in resolving the visible problems of the day. This whole approach is too fortuitous and the situation too specific to bear usefully on anything so fundamental as authentic progress. Apparent adequacy relative to the existing body of knowledge (which, after all, is the best we can do in this direction) is a very myopic guide.

The lesson of these considerations is simply that the perceived adequacy of science reflected in the relationship of question sets is a roller coaster that affords little useful insight into the fundamentals of scientific progress.

4. Quality Poses Problems

It is time to step back from the proliferation of doctrines relating progress to size comparisons among question agendas and view the matter from a different perspective. The salient point is that even if the historical course of scientific inquiry had in fact conformed, overall, to one or another of the patterns of question-answer dialectic envisaged by these various theories, this circumstance would simply be fortuitous. It would not reflect any deep principle inherent in the very nature of the enterprise. For the common failing of *all* the approaches to progress that we have been considering is that they deal (in the first instance, at any rate) simply with questions as such, without worrying about their *significance*. To render such theories at all meaningful, this factor would have to be reckoned with. The theory would have to be construed as applying not to questions per se but to *important* questions—questions at or above some suitable level of significance.

Now, the "importance" of a factual question Q, turns in the final analysis on how substantial a revision in our body of scientific beliefs S is wrought by our grappling with it, that is, the extent to which answering it causes geological tremors across the cognitive landscape. But two very different sorts of things can be at issue here: either a mere *expansion* of S by additions, or, more seriously, a *revision* of it that involves *replacing* some of its members and readjusting the remainder so as to restore overall consistency. This second sort of change in a body of knowledge, its *revision* rather than mere *augmentation,* is, in general, the more significant matter, and a question whose resolution forces revisions is likely to be of greater significance than one that merely fills in some part of the *terra incognita* of knowledge. However—and this is crucial—the fact of the matter is that the magnitude of the transformation from an earlier S_1 to a later successor S_2 can only be retrospectively assessed once we have actually arrived at S_2.

The crucial point is that progressiveness, insignificance, importance, interest, and the like are all state-of-the-art relative conceptions. To apply these ideas, we must *already* have a particular scientific corpus in hand to provide a vantage point for their assessment. No commitment-neutral basis is available for deciding whether S_1 is progressive vis-à-vis S_2 or the reverse. If the test of a theory is to be its problem-solving capacity—its capacity to provide viable answers to *interesting* and *important* questions[10]—then merely quantitative considerations that prescind from quality will not be up to doing the job.

This issue of quality is the sticking point. The *importance* or *interest* of a question that arises in one state-of-the-art is something that can only be discovered with hindsight from the vantage point of the new bodies of knowledge S to which the attempts to grapple with it had led us. In science, apparently insignificant problems (the blue color of the sky or the anomalous excess of background radiation) can acquire great importance once we have a state-of-the-art that makes them instances of important new effects that instantiate or indicate major theoretical innovations. To reemphasize, the importance of questions is something that we can only assess with the wisdom of scientific hindsight. Accordingly, to secure an adequate standard of progressiveness, we had best look in an altogether different direction, going back to square one and beginning with fundamentals.

5. The Exploration Model and Its Implications

Natural science is not a fixed object—a finished product of our inquiries—but an ongoing process. In developing natural science, we humans began by exploring the world in our own locality, and not just our spatial neighborhood but, more far-reachingly, in our *parametric* neighborhood in the space of physical variable such as temperature, pressure, and electrical charge. Near the "home base" of the state of things in our accustomed natural environment, we can operate with relative ease and freedom—thanks to the evolutionary attunement of our sensory and cognitive apparatus—in scanning nature with the unassisted senses for data regarding its modes of operation. But in due course we accomplish everything that can be managed by these straightforward means. To do more, we have to "explore" further—to extend our probes into nature more deeply, deploying increasing technical sophistication to achieve more and more demanding levels of interactive capability, moving ever further away from our evolutionary home base in nature toward increasingly remote observational frontiers. From the egocentric starting point of our local region of parameter space, we journey outward to explore nature's various parametric dimensions ever more distantly. It is the very essence of the enterprise that natural science is forced to press into ever remoter reaches of parametric space.

This picture is not, of course, one of *geographical* exploration but rather of the physical exploration—and subsequent theoretical systematization—of phenomena distributed over the parametric space of nature's physical dimensions. This approach to exploratory processes provides a conception of scientific research as prospecting for the phenomena required for significant, new scientific findings. As the range of telescopes, the energy of particle accelerators, the effectiveness of low-temperature instrumentation, the potency of pressurization equipment, the power of vacuum-creating contrivances, and the accuracy of measurement apparatus increase—that is, as our capacity to move about in the parametric space of the physical world is enhanced—new phenomena come into view. After the major findings accessible through the data of a given level of technological sophistication have been achieved, further major findings become realizable only when one ascends to the next level of sophistication in data-relevant technology. Thus the key to the great progress of contemporary physics lies in the enormous strides that have been made in technological capability.[11]

No doubt, nature is in itself uniform in its distribution of diverse processes across the reaches of parameter space. It does not favor us by clustering them in our own natural parametric vicinity. However, *cognitively* significant phenomena in fact become increasingly sparse because the scientific mind has the capacity to do so much so well early on. Our power of theoretical triangulation is so great that we can make a disproportionately effective use of the phenomena located in our local parametric neighborhood. In consequence, scientific innovation becomes more and more difficult—and expensive—as we push out farther and father from our evolutionary home base toward ever more remote frontiers. After the major findings accessible at a given capacity level in data-relevant technology have been achieved, further major findings become realizable when one ascends to a higher level of sophistication. We confront a situation of technological escalation. The need for new data constrains looking further and further from man's familiar "home base" in the parametric space of nature. Thus, while further significant scientific progress is in principle always possible—there being no absolute or intrinsic limits of significantly novel facts—the *realization* of this ongoing prospect for scientific discovery demands a continual enhancement in the technological state-of-the-art of data extraction or exploitation.

This ever more far-reaching exploration of the parametric spectra associated with different conditions in nature demands continual increases in physical power. To enable our experimental apparatus to realize greater velocities, higher frequencies, lower or higher temperatures, greater pressures, larger energy excitations, stabler conditions, or greater resolving power, and so on, requires ever more powerful equipment capable of continually more enhanced performance. The *sort* of "power" at issue will, of course, vary with the nature of the particular parametric dimension under consideration—be it velocity, frequency, or temperature—but the general principle remains the same. Scientific progress depends crucially and unavoidably on our technical capability to penetrate the increasingly distant, and increasingly difficult, reaches of the power-complexity spectrum of physical parameters, to explore and to explain the ever more remote phenomena encountered there. Only by operating under new, previously inaccessible conditions of observational or experimental interactions with nature—attaining ever more extreme temperature, pressure, particle velocity, field strength, and so on—can we bring new impetus to scientific progress.

This idea of the exploration of parametric space provides a basic model for understanding the mechanism of scientific innovation in mature natural science. New technology increases the range of access within the parametric space of physical processes. Such increased access brings new phenomena to light, and the examination and theoretical accommodation of these phenomena is the basis for growth in our scientific understanding of nature. As an army marches on its "stomach" (its logistical support), so science depends upon it "eyes"—it is crucially dependent on the technological instrumentalities that constitute the sources of its data. Natural science is fundamentally *empirical,* and its advance is critically dependent not on human ingenuity alone but on the monitoring observations to which we can only gain access through interactions with nature. The days are long past when useful scientific data can be gathered by unaided sensory observation of the ordinary course of nature. *Artifice* has become an indispensable route to the acquisition and processing of scientifically useful data: the sorts of data on which scientific discovery nowadays depends can only be generated by technological means.

We arrive therefore at the situation of *technological escalation.* The need for new data forces us to look further and further in parametric space. For though scientific progress is, in principle, always possible—there being no absolute or intrinsic limits to significant scientific discovery—the realization of this ongoing prospect demands a continual enhancement in the technological state-of-the-art of data extraction or exploitation. In science, as in a technological arms race, one is simply never called on to keep doing what was done before. One is always forced further up the mountain, ascending to ever higher levels of technological performance—and of expense.

Without an ever-developing process of technological advance, scientific progress would grind to a halt. The discoveries of today cannot be advanced with yesterday's instrumentation and techniques. To secure new observations, to test new hypotheses, and to detect new phenomena, an ever more powerful technology of inquiry is needed. Throughout the natural sciences, technological progress is a crucial requisite for cognitive progress. We have embarked on an endless endeavor to improve the range of effective observational and experimental intervention. Only by operating under new and previously inaccessible conditions—attaining extreme temperature, pressure, particle velocity, field strength, and so on—can we realize those circumstances that enable us to put our hypotheses and theories to the test. As an acute observer has rightly remarked, "Most critical experiments [in physics] planned today, if they had to be constrained within the technology of even ten years ago, would be seriously compromised."[12]

The salient characteristic of this situation is that, once the major findings accessible at a given level of sophistication have been attained, further major progress in any given problem area requires ascent to a higher level on the technological scale. Every data-technology level is subject to discovery saturation, but the exhaustion of prospects at a given level does not, of course, bring progress to a halt. Once the potential of a given state-of-the-art level has been exploited, not all our piety or wit can lure the technological frontier back to yield further significant returns at this stage. Further substantive findings become realizable only by enhancing our sophistication in data-relevant technology. As science endeavors to extend its "mastery over nature," it becomes enmeshed in a technology-intensive arms race against nature, with all of the practical and economic implications characteristic of such process.

6. Theorizing as Inductive Projection

Theorizing in natural science is a matter of triangulation from observations—of making leaps of inductive generalization from the data. And (sensibly enough) induction as a rational process of inquiry constructs the simplest, most economical cognitive structures to house these data comfortably. It calls for searching out the simplest pattern of regularity that can adequately accommodate our data regarding the issues at hand and then projects them globally across the entire spectrum of possibilities in order to answer our general questions. Accordingly, scientific theorizing, as a fundamentally inductive process, involves the search for, or the construction of, the least complex theory structure capable of accommodating the available body of data—proceeding under the aegis of established principles of inductive systematization: uniformity, simplicity, harmony, and such principles that implement the general idea of cognitive economy. Directly evidential considerations apart, the warrant of inductively authorized contentions turns exactly on this issue of how efficiently and effectively they coordinate data—on consilience, mutual interconnection, and systemic enmeshment. Induction is a matter of building up the simplest theory structure capable of "doing the job" of explanatory systematization. The key

principle is that of simplicity, and the ruling injunction that of cognitive economy. Complications cannot be ruled out, but they must always
pay their way in terms of increased systemic adequacy.

Simplicity and generality are the cornerstones of inductive systematization. One very important point must be stressed in this connection.
The basic idea in scientific induction of a *coordinative systematization of
question-resolving conjecture with the data of experience* may sound like a
very conservative process. But this impression would be quite incorrect.
The drive to systematization embodies an imperative to broaden the
range of our experience—to extend and to expand as far as possible the
data base from which our theoretical triangulations proceed. In the
design of cognitive systems, implicity/harmony and comprehensive-
ness/inclusiveness are the two sides of a unified whole. The impetus toward ever ampler comprehensiveness indicates why the ever-widening
exploration of nature's parameter space is an indispensable part of the
process.

With the enhancement of scientific technology, the size and complexity of this body of data inevitably grow, expanding in quantity and
diversifying in kind. Technological progress constantly enlarges the
window through which we look out on nature's parametric space. In
developing natural science, we continually enlarge our view of this
space and then generalize upon what we see. But what we have here is
not a homogeneous lunar landscape, where once we have seen one sector we have seen it all, and where theory projections from lesser data
generally remain in place when further data come our way.

Our exploration of physical parameter space is inevitably incomplete. We can never exhaust the whole range of temperatures, pressures, particle velocities, and so forth. And so we inevitably face the
(very real) prospect that the regularity structure of the as-yet-inaccessi-
ble cases will not conform to the (generally simpler) patterns of regularity prevailing in the presently accessible cases. By and large, future
data do not accommodate themselves to present theories. Newtonian

calculations worked marvelously for predicting solar-system phenomenology (eclipses, planetary conjunctions, and the rest), but this does not show that classical physics has no need for fundamental revision. Historical experience shows that there is every reason to expect that our ideas about nature are subject to constant radical changes as we explore parametric space more extensively. The technologically mediated entry into new regions of parameter space constantly destabilizes the attained equilibrium between data and theory.

The theoretical claims of science are not spatiotemporally localized, and they are not parametrically localized either. They stipulate, quite ambitiously, how things are always and everywhere. It does not require a sophisticated knowledge of history of science to see that our worst fears are usually realized or that it is seldom if ever the case that our theories survive intact in the wake of substantial extensions in our access to sectors of parametric space. The history of science is a history of episodes of leaping to the wrong conclusions.

At each stage of inquiry in physical science we try to embed the phenomena and their regularities within the simplest (cognitively most efficient) explanatory fabric to answer our questions about the world and to guide our interactions in it. Breadth of coverage in point of data and economy of means in point of theory are our guiding stars.

Against this background let us contemplate an analogy. Let us suppose that we investigate some domain of phenomena on such a basis, and that in the first instance the picture we arrive at is one showing a certain sort of regularity as shown here:

We say, "Aha, this sector of the world's processes proceeds in the manner of a mountain range." But at the next level we investigate those zigzags more closely. We note now that they have the following distinctly more complex form:

We say, "So—we did not quite have it right to begin with. This sector of the world's processes actually has the character of fluctuating castellations." And so, at the next level we investigate those castellations more closely. We now note that they, in turn, have changed form:

We now say, "Aha, this sector of the world is made up of regularly configured zigzags." And so this sort of observation-driven revisionism continues at every successive stage of further technological sophistication in our experimental and observational interactions with physical nature. At every level of detail, nature's apparent modus operandi looks very different, and its "governing regularities" take on an aspect markedly different from what went before and crucially disparate from it.

Note, however, that at each stage we can readily comprehend and explain the situation of the earlier stage. We can always say, "Yes, of course, given that that is how things stand, it is quite understandable that earlier on, when we proceeded in such-and-such a cruder way, we arrived at the sort of findings we did—incorrect and inaccurate though they are." But, of course, this wisdom is one of hindsight only. At no stage do we have the prospect of using *foresight* to predict what lies ahead. The impossibility of foreseeing the new phenomena that awaits us means that at no point can we prejudge what lies further down the explanatory road.

Let us now turn from a concern with the *lawful comportment* of the world's phenomena to the *constitution* of its things. An analogy may prove helpful. Suppose we initially investigate objects of a certain type. Proceeding at the first level of sophistication we see them as constituted of parts whose structure is O-like. However, on closer investigation we find (at the next level of sophistication) that these "component parts" were not actually units but mere constellations, mere clouds of small specks as per ⁙ . But when we investigate still more deeply, it emerges that the component specks that constitute these "clouds" themselves have the rectangular form ▭. Suppose further that at the next level those rectangular "components" themselves emerge as mere constellations, composed of triangular constituents of the form Δ, and so on. As this analogy indicates, physical nature can exhibit a very different aspect when viewed from the vantage point of different levels of sophistication in the technology of the nature-investigator interaction.

Thus regarding both the observable *regularities* of nature and the discernible *constituents* of nature, very different results that invite very different views of the situation can, and almost invariably do, emerge at successive levels of the observational state-of-the-art. Almost invariably we deal at every stage with a different order or aspect of things. The reason why nature exhibits different aspects at different levels is not that nature itself is somehow stratified in its makeup but that (1) the character of the available nature-investigative interactions is variable and differs from level to level of sophistication in matters of inquiry, and (2) the character of the "findings" at which one arrives will hinge on the character of these nature-investigative interactions. What we detect or "find" in nature always depends on the mechanisms by which we search. The phenomena we detect will depend not merely on nature's operations alone but on the physical and conceptional instrumentalities that we ourselves deploy in investigating nature. For as Bacon saw, nature will never tell us more than we can forcibly extract from it with the means of interaction at our disposal. What we can manage to extract by successively deeper probes is bound to wear a steadily changing aspect.

As noted earlier, Newton's third law of countervailing action and reaction becomes a fundamental principle of epistemology because we can only learn about nature by interacting with it. Everything depends on just how and *how hard* we can push against nature in situations of observational and detectional interaction. We cannot "get to the bottom of it" where nature is concerned. Nature always has hidden reserves of power. Successive stages in the technological state-of-the-art of scientific inquiry thus lead us to different views about the nature of things and the character of their laws. But the sequence of successively more powerful and sophisticated instrumentalities on the side of inquirers need not be matched by any coordinated succession of layers in the constitution of physical existence somehow captured "correctly" by our inquiry at corresponding levels of sophistication. The "layers" we encounter principally reflect our own procedures.

Accordingly, it is a wholly unwarranted supposition that there is a sequence of nature levels placed conveniently alongside our inquiry levels, in parallel coordination, that makes for an elegantly ladderlike configuration. Nature just goes along "doing its thing." Nature has no layers, no differentiated physical strata of levels.[13] The only physical levels are process-relative, hinging on the character of our technologically mediated modes of observation and manipulation.

7. Scientific Revolutions as Potentially Unending

Some theorists regard science as an essentially closed venture that will ultimately come to the end of its tether. They see the scientific project as an inherently bounded venture, subject to the idea that since nature is governed by a finite family of fundamental laws, it follows that in scientific inquiry, as in the geographical exploration of the planet, we are ultimately bound to reach the end of the road.[14] But this position is eminently problematic. There is good reason to think of nature as cognitively inexhaustible: as we extend the range of our interactions, we can, in theory, always learn more and more about it, attaining ever new horizons of discovery, with the new no less interesting or significant than the old.

This perspective on the processes that underlie the development of science has important implications. It means that science cannot be a complete *system,* a finished structure of knowledge, but is and will ever remain a *process*—an inquiring activity whose ultimate goal may be the completion of a finished and perfected system, but which proceeds in the full recognition that this aim is ultimately unreachable. Neither theoretical issues of general principle nor the actualities of historical experience suggest that scientific progress need ever come to a stop.[15] Of course, it is possible that for reasons of exhaustion, of penury, or of discouragement, we humans might cease to push the frontiers forward. Should we ever abandon the journey, however, it will be for reasons such as these and not because we have reached the end of the road.

But how can unlimited scientific discovery be possible? To underwrite the prospect of endless progress in the development of natural science, some theoreticians deem it necessary to stipulate an intrinsic infinitude in the makeup of nature as a physical structure makeup of nature itself.[16] The physicist David Bohm, for example, writes, "at least as a working hypothesis science assumes the infinity of nature; and this assumption fits the facts much better than any other point of view that we know."[17] Bohm and his congeners thus postulate an infinite quantitative scope or an infinite qualitative diversity in nature, assuming either a principle of unending intricacy in its makeup or one of unending orders of spatiostructural nesting. But is this sort of thing needed at all? Does the prospect of potentially limitless scientific progress actually require structural infinitude in the physical composition of nature along some such lines? The answer is surely negative.

The prime task of science lies in discovering the laws of nature, and it is law complexity that is crucial for this purpose.[18] Even the workings of a structurally finite and indeed simple system can yet exhibit an infinite intricacy in operational or functional complexity, exhibiting this limitless complexity in its workings rather than at the spatiostructural or compositional level. While the number of constituents of nature may be small, the ways in which they may be combined can be infinite. Think of the examples of letters, syllables, words, sentences, paragraphs, different sorts of books, libraries, and library systems. There is no need to assume a "ceiling" to such a sequence of levels of integrative complexity. The emergence of new concept-concatenations and new laws can be expected at every stage. Each level exhibits its own order. The laws we attain at the nth level can have features whose investigation lifts us to the $(n + 1)$ level. New phenomena and new laws can arise at every new level of integrative order. Knowing the frequency with which individual letters like A and T occur in a text will not tell us much about the frequency with which a combination such as AT occurs. When we change the purview of our conceptual horizons, there is always, in principle, more to be learned. The different facets of nature can generate new strata of laws that yield a potentially unending sequence of levels, each giving rise to its own characteristic principles of organization, themselves quite unpredictable from the standpoint of the other levels.

The usual recourse to an infinity-of-nature principle is strictly one-sided, placing the burden of responsibility for the endlessness of science solely on the shoulders of nature itself. According to this view, the potential endlessness of scientific progress requires limitlessness on the side of its *objects*, so that the infinitude of nature must be postulated either at the structural or at the functional levels. But this is a mistake.

Science, the cognitive exploration of the ways of the world, is a matter of the *interaction* of the mind with the nature of the *mind's ex-*

ploitation of the data to which it gains access in order to penetrate the "secrets of nature." The crucial fact is that scientific progress hinges not just on the structure of nature but also on the structure of the information-acquiring processes by which we investigate it.

Ongoing cognitive innovation thus need not be provided for by assuming (as a "working hypothesis" or otherwise) that the system being investigated is infinitely complex in its physical or functional makeup. It suffices to hypothesize an endlessly ongoing prospect of securing fuller information about it. The salient point is that *cognitive* rather than structural or operational complexity is the key here. After all, even when a scene is itself only finitely complex, an ever ampler view of it will come to realization as the resolving power of our conceptual and observational instruments is increased. Responsibility, therefore, for the open-endedness of science need not lie on the side of nature at all but can rest one-sidedly with us, its explorers. When we make measurements to accuracy A, the world may appear X_1-wise; and when to accuracy $(1/2)A$ it may appear X_2-wise; and when to accuracy $(1/2^n)A$ it may appear X_n-wise. At each successive state-of-the-art stage of increased precision in our investigative proceedings, the world may take on a very different nomic appearance, not because it changes, but simply because at each state it *presents* itself differently to us.

Accordingly, the question of the ongoing progressiveness of science should not be confined to a consideration of nature alone, since the character of our information-gathering procedures, as channeled through our theoretical perspectives, is also bound to play a crucial part.[19] Innovations on the side of data can generate new theories, and new theories can transform the very meaning of the old data. This dialectical process of successive feedback has no inherent limits and suffices to underwrite a prospect of ongoing innovation. Even a finite nature can, like a typewriter with a limited keyboard, yield an endlessly varied text. It can produce a steady stream of *new* data—"new" not necessarily in kind but in their functional interrelationships and thus in their theoretical implications—on the basis of which our knowledge of nature's operative laws is continually enhanced and deepened.

These various considerations combine to indicate that *an assumption of the quantitative infinity of the physical extent of the natural universe or of the qualitative infinity of its structural complexity is simply not required to provide for the prospects of ongoing scientific progress.* Ongoing discovery is as much a matter of how we inquirers proceed with our work as it is of the object of inquiry itself. This fact constrains us to recognize that even a finitely complex nature can provide the domain for a virtually endless course of new and significant discovery. There is no good reason to think that the natural science of a finite world is an inherently closed and terminable venture, and there is no adequate basis for the view that the search for greater "depth" in our understanding must eventually terminate at a logical end.[20] By all indications, historical as well as theoretical, the prospect of ongoing "scientific revolutions" is potentially unending. Scientific inquiry, in sum, is a potentially endless process.

8. Is Later Lesser?

Some theorists find it tempting to follow Peirce in seeing the ongoing process of scientific change as tending to be a fixed and stable product by way of *convergent approximation.*[21] This view calls for envisaging a situation where, with the passage of time, the results we reach grow increasingly concordant and the outcomes attained become less and less differentiated. In the face of such a course of successive changes of ever-diminishing significance, the reality of ongoing change is now irrelevant since with the passage of time the changes matter less and less. We increasingly approximate an essentially stable picture. This prospect is certainly a theoretically possible one. But neither historical experience nor considerations of general principle provide reason to think that it is actually possible. Instead, quite the reverse!

Any theory of convergence in science, however carefully crafted, will shatter under the impact of the *conceptual innovation* that becomes necessary to deal with the new phenomena encountered in the wake of technical escalation. Such innovation continually brings entirely new, radically different scientific concepts to the fore, carrying in its wake an ongoing wholesale revision of "established fact." New and different concepts are just that—new and different; there just is no issue of degree here.

Ongoing scientific progress is not simply a matter of increasing accuracy by extending the numbers at issue in our otherwise stable descriptions of nature out to a few more decimal places. Significant scientific progress is genuinely revolutionary in involving a *fundamental change of mind* about how things happen in the world. Progress of this caliber is generally a matter not of adding further facts—on the order of filling in a crossword puzzle. It is, rather, a matter of changing the very framework itself. And this fact blocks the theory of convergence.

In any convergent process, *later* is *lesser*. But since scientific progress on matters of fundamental importance is generally a matter of replacement rather than mere supplementation, there is no good reason for seeing the later findings of science as less significant within the cognitive enterprise than earlier findings—that is, to think that nature will be cooperative in always yielding its most important secrets early on and reserving nothing but the relatively insignificant for later. (Nor does it seem plausible to think of nature as perverse, luring us ever more deeply into deception as inquiry proceeds.) A very small scale effect at the level of phenomena—even one that lies at the outer extremes of a "range exploration" in terms of temperature, pressure, velocity, or the like—can force a far-reaching revolution and have a profound impact through major theoretical revisions. (Think of special relativity in relation to ether-drift experimentation, or general relativity in relation to the perihelion of Mercury.) To all those late-nineteenth-century physicists who investigated the properties of the luminiferous ether, the prospect that a medium might not exist for the transmission of light and electromagnetism was unrealistic.

Given that natural science progresses mainly by substitutions and replacements that involve comprehensive overall revisions of our picture of the processes at issue, it seems sensible to say that the shifts across successive scientific "revolutions" maintain the same level of overall significance when taken as a whole. At the cognitive level, a scientific innovation is simply a matter of change. Scientific progress is neither a convergent nor a divergent process.[22] It is a matter of ongoing change, confronting us with a situation in which every major successive stage in the evolution of science yields innovations, and these innovations are, on the whole, of roughly equal *overall* interest and importance. Accordingly, we have little alternative but to reject a convergentism of increasingly minor readjustments as a position that lacks the support not only of considerations of general principles but also of the actual realities of our experience in the history of science. If substantive convergentism does not do justice to the scope of the processes at work in scientific progress, where then are we to look?

9. Applicative Efficacy as the Key to Progress

Applicative praxis—not theoretical merit but practical capability—is the best available standard for assessing scientific progress. Clearly, the most promising prospect calls for approaching the issue of scientific progress in terms of *pragmatic* rather than strictly *cognitive* standards. As seen from the angle of such an approach, progressively superior science does not manifest itself as such through the sophistication of its theories (for, after all, even absurd theories can be made very complex), but through the superiority of its applications as judged by the old Bacon-Hobbes standard of *scientia propter potentiam*—that is, through affording us increased power of prediction and control. This means that, in the end, *praxis* is the arbiter of theory. To understand scientific progress and its limits, we must look not toward the cognitive dialectic of questions and answers but toward the scope and limits of human power in our interactions with nature. To progress we must, in sum, look not so much to what we can *say* as to what we can *do*. The pragmatic dimension is paramount.

An instructive lesson emerges from these deliberations. Scientific knowledge is not a fixed structure but a process. Our knowledge of ourselves and of the world about us is always a work in progress because our capacity to answer questions is limited. But beyond this there is even a limited significance to the whole business of question resolution. Even substantial success along these lines need not by itself betoken real progress in the project of advancing our understanding of how things really work in the world. Instead, progress becomes manifest through greater power—in improved technology; the crux lies in enhancing the range of our practice. Successful application is the key: superior science is as superior science does when and as it establishes its superiority through its greater operational effectiveness. Knowledge development is a process both fueled by and manifested through our technologically mediated capabilities for interacting with nature.

CHAPTER SIX

The Cognitive Process and Metaphysical Realism

1. Hidden Depths: The Impetus to Realism

The circumstance that our factual knowledge of the world's arrangements is a process of ongoing interaction with nature has far-reaching implications. It means that as far as we finite knowers are concerned, real things have hidden depths—they are always cognitively opaque to us to some extent because more about them can always come to light.

Any particular thing—the moon, for example—is such that two related but critically different versions can be contemplated: (1) the moon, the actual moon as it "really" is; and (2) the moon as somebody (you or I or the Babylonians) conceives of it. The crucial fact is that the thing we *intend* to communicate or think (self-communicate) about is virtually always the former item—the thing *as it is*—and not first the thing *as somebody conceives of it*—ourselves included. Yet we cannot but recognize the justice of Kant's teaching that the "I think" (I maintain, I assert) is an ever present, implicit accompaniment of every claim or contention that we make. This factor of attributability dogs our every assertion and opens up the unavoidable prospect of "getting it wrong."

However, this fundamental objectivity-intent—the determination to discuss "the moon itself" (the real moon) regardless of how untenable one's own *ideas* about it may eventually prove to be—is a basic precondition of the very possibility of communication. It is crucial to the communicative enterprise to take the egocentrism-avoiding stance of an epistemological Copernicanism that rejects all claims to a privileged status for *our own* conception of things. Such a conviction roots in the fact that we are prepared to "discount any misconceptions" (our own included) about things over a very wide range indeed—that we are committed to the stance that factual disagreements as to the character of things are communicatively irrelevant within enormously broad limits.

We are able to say something about the (real) Sphinx because of our submission to a fundamental communicative convention or "social contract": to the effect that we *intend* ("mean") to talk about it, the very thing itself as it "really" is, our own private conception of it notwithstanding. We arrive at the standard policy that prevails in all communicative discourse of letting "the language we use," rather than whatever specific informative aims we may actually "have in mind" on particular occasions, be the decisive factor regarding the things at issue in our discourse. When I speak about the Sphinx—even though I do so based on my own conception of what is involved here—I will nevertheless be taken to be discussing "the *real* Sphinx" by virtue of the basic conventionalized intention at issue regarding the operation of referring terms.

Communication requires not only common *concepts* but also common *topics,* that is, shared items of discussion, a common world of self-subsistently real "*an sich*" objects basic to shared experience. The factor of objectivity reflects our basic commitment to a shared world as the common property of communicators. Such a commitment involves more than merely de facto intersubjective agreement. Such agreement is a matter of a posteriori discovery, whereas our view of the nature of things puts "the real world" on a necessary and a priori basis. This stance is rooted in the fundamental convention of a socially shared insistence on communicating—that is, the commitment to an objective world of real things affording the crucially requisite common focus needed for any genuine communication.

Any pretentions to the predominance, let alone the correctness, of our own conceptions regarding the furniture of this realm must be put aside in the context of communication. The fundamental intention to deal with the objective order of this "real world" is crucial. If our assertoric commitments did not transcend the information we ourselves have on hand, we would never be able to "get in touch" with others about a shared objective world. No claim is made for the *primacy* of our conceptions, or for the *correctness* of our conceptions, or even for the mere *agreement* of our conceptions with those of others. The fundamental intention to discuss "the thing itself" predominates and overrides any mere dealing with the thing as we ourselves conceive of it.

If we were to set up our own conception as somehow definitive and decisive, we would at once erect a grave impediment to the prospect of successful communication with one another. Communication could then only proceed retrospectively with the wisdom of hindsight. It would be realized only in the implausible case that extensive exchange indicates that there has been an *identity* of conceptions all along. We would then learn only by experience—at the end of a long process of wholly tentative and provisional exchange. We would always stand on very shaky ground. For no matter how far we pushed our inquiry into the issue of an identity of conceptions, the prospect of a divergence lying just around the corner—waiting to be discovered if only we pursued the matter just a bit further—could never be precluded. One could never advance the issue of identity of focus beyond the status of a more or less well-grounded *assumption*. Any so-called communication would no longer be an exchange of information but a tissue of frail conjectures. The communicative enterprise would become a vast inductive project—a complex exercise in theory building, leading tentatively and provisionally toward something that, in fact, the imputational groundwork of our language enables us to presuppose from the very outset.[1]

To be sure, someone might object: "But surely we can get by on the basis of personal conceptions alone, without invoking the notion of 'a thing itself.' My conception of a thing is something I can convey to you, given enough time. Cannot communication proceed by correlating and matching personal conceptions, without appeal to the intermediation of 'the thing itself.'?" But think here of the concrete practicalities. What is "enough time"? When is the match "sufficient" to underwrite our right identification? The cash value of our commitment to the thing itself is that it enables us to make this identification straight away by imputation, by fiat on the basis of modest indicators, rather than on the basis of an appeal to the inductive weight of a body of evidence that is always bound to be problematic. Communication is something *we set out* to do, not something we ultimately discern, with the wisdom of eventual hindsight, to have accomplished retrospectively.

Nevertheless, these objections make a useful contribution. They engender recognition that "the thing itself" operative in this discussion is not a peculiar sort of *thing*—a new ontological category—but rather a shorthand formula that encapsulates a certain policy of communicative presumption or imputation, namely that of an a priori commitment to the idea of a commonality of objective focus that is to be allowed to stand unless and until circumstances arise to render this untenable.

The objectifying imputation at issue here lies at the very basis of our cognitive stance that we live and operate in a world of real and objective things. This commitment to the idea of a shared real world is crucial for communication. Its status is a priori: its existence is not something we learn of through experience. As Kant clearly saw, objective experience is possible only if the existence of such a real, objective world is *presupposed* at the onset rather than seen as a matter of ex post facto discovery about the nature of things.

The information that we may have about a thing—be it real or presumptive information—is always just that, namely, information that *we* lay claim to. We cannot but recognize that it is person-relative and in general person-differentiated. Our attempts at communication and inquiry are thus undergirded by an information-transcending stance—the stance that we communally inhabit a shared world of objectively existing things, a world of "real things" among which we live and into which we inquire but about which we do and must presume ourselves to have only imperfect information at any and every particular stage of the cognitive venture. This is not something we learn. The "facts of experience" can never reveal it to us. It is something we postulate or presuppose. Its epistemic status is not that of an empirical discovery but that of a presupposition that is a product of a transcendental argument for the very possibility of communication or inquiry as we standardly conceive of them.

And so, what is at issue here is not a matter of *discovery*, but one of *imputation*. The element of community, of identity of focus, is not a matter of ex post facto learning from experience, but of an a priori predetermination inherent in our approach to language use. We do not *infer* things as being real and objective from our phenomenal data but establish our perception as authentic perception *of* genuine objects through the fact that these objects are given—or, rather, *taken*—as real and objectively existing things from the outset.[2] Objectivity is not deduced but imputed.

It is crucial that the mechanisms of human communication should lie within the domain of human power—they could not otherwise be what they are. Now with respect to the *meanings of words*, this condition is satisfied, because this is something that we ourselves fix by custom or by fiat. But *the correctness of conceptions* is not simply a matter of human discretion—it is something that lies outside the sphere of our effective control. For a "correct conception" is akin to Spinoza's *true idea* of which he stipulates that it must "agree with its object" in circumstances where this issue of agreement may well elude us.[3] (Humans propose but do not dispose with respect to this matter of idea/actuality coordination.) We do, no doubt, *purport* our conceptions to be correct, but whether this is indeed so is something we cannot tell with assurance until "all the returns are in"—that is, never. This fact renders it critically important *that* (and understandable *why*) conceptions are communicatively irrelevant. Our discourse *reflects* our conceptions and perhaps *conveys* them, but it is not substantive *about* them.

We thus reach an important conjuncture of ideas. The ontological independence of things—their objectivity and autonomy of the machinations of mind—is a crucial aspect of realism. The fact that it lies at the very core of our conception of a real thing such that items project beyond the cognitive reach of mind betokens a conceptual scheme fundamentally committed to objectivity. The only plausible sort of ontology is one that contemplates a realm of reality that outruns the range of knowledge (and even of language), adopting the stance that character goes beyond the limits of characterization. It is a salient aspect of the mind-independent status of the objectively real that the features of something real always transcend what we know about it. Indeed, yet further or different facts concerning a real thing can always come to light, and all that we *do* say about it does not exhaust all that *can and should* be said about it. In this light, objectivity is crucial to realism, and the cognitive inexhaustibility of things is a certain token of their objectivity.

2. The Pragmatic Foundation of Realism as a Basis for Communication and Discourse

But what is it, brute necessity aside, that validates those communicative presuppositions and postulations of ours? The prime factor at work here is simply our commitment to utility. Given that the existence of an objective domain of impersonally real existence is not a *product* of but a *precondition* for empirical inquiry, its acceptance has to be validated in the manner appropriate for postulates and prejudgments of any sort—namely, in terms of its ultimate utility. Bearing this pragmatic perspective in mind, let us take a closer look at this issue of utility and ask, What can this postulation of a mind-independent reality actually do for us?

The answer is straightforward. The assumption of a mind-independent reality is essential to the whole of our standard conceptual scheme relating to inquiry and communications. Without it, both the actual conduct and the rational legitimation of our communicative and investigative (evidential) practice would be destroyed. Nothing that we do in this cognitive domain would make sense if we did not subscribe to the conception of a mind-independent reality.

First, we indispensably require the notion of reality to operate within the classical conception of truth as "agreement with reality" *(adaequatio ad rem)*. Once we abandon the concept of reality, the idea that in accepting a factual claim as true we become committed to how matters actually stand—"how it really is"—would also go by the board. The very semantics of our discourse constrain its commitment to realism; we have no alternative but to regard as real those states of affairs claimed by the contentions we are prepared to accept. Once we put a contention forward by way of serious assertion, we must view as real the states of affairs it purports and must see its claims as facts. We need the notion of reality to operate the conception of truth. A factual statement on the order of "There are pi mesons" is true if and only if the world is such that pi mesons exist within it. By virtue of their very nature as truths, true statements must state facts: they state what really is so, which is exactly what it is to "characterize reality." The conceptions of *truth* and of *reality* come together in the notion of *adaequatio ad rem*—the venerable principle that to speak truly is to say how matters stand in reality, in that things actually are as we have said them to be.

Second, the nihilistic denial that there is such a thing as reality would destroy once and for all the crucial Parmenidean divide between appearance and reality. And it would exact a fearful price from us: we would be reduced to talking only of what we (I, you, many of us) *think* to be so. The crucial contrast notion of the *real* truth would no longer be available: we would only be able to contrast our *putative* truths with those of others but could no longer operate the classical distinction between the putative and the actual, between what people merely *think* to be so and what actually *is* so. We could not take the stance that, as the Aristotelian commentator Themistius put it, "that which exists does not conform to various opinions, but rather the correct opinions conform to that which exists."[4]

The third point is the issue of cognitive coordination. Communication and inquiry, as we actually carry them out, are predicated on the fundamental idea of a real world of objective things, existing and functioning "in themselves," without specific dependence on us and so equally accessible to others. Intersubjectively valid communication can only be based on common access to an objective order of things. The whole communicative project is predicated on a commitment to the idea that there is a realm of shared objects about which we as a community share questions and beliefs, and about which we ourselves as individuals presumably have only imperfect information that can be criticized and augmented by the efforts of others.

This points to a fourth important consideration. Only through reference to the real world as a *common object* and shared focus of our diverse and imperfect epistemic strivings are we able to effect communicative contact with one another. Inquiry and communication alike are geared to the conception of an objective world: a communally shared realm of things that exist strictly "on their own" comprising an enduring and independent realm within which and, more importantly, with reference to which inquiry proceeds. We could not proceed on the basis of the notion that inquiry estimates the character of the real if we were not prepared to presume or postulate a reality for these estimates to be estimates of. It would clearly be pointless to devise our characterizations of reality if we did not stand committed to the proposition that there is a reality to be characterized.

The fifth item is a recourse to mind-independent reality that makes possible a "realistic" view of our knowledge as potentially flawed. A rejection of this commitment to reality *an sich* (or to the actual truth about it) exacts an unacceptable price. For in abandoning this commitment we also lose those regulative contrasts that canalize and condition our view of the nature of inquiry (and indeed shape our conception of this process as it stands within the framework of our conceptual scheme). We could no longer assert: "What we have there is good enough as far as it goes, but it is presumably not the 'whole real truth' of the matter." The very conception of inquiry as we conceive it would have to be abandoned if the contract conceptions of "actual reality" and "the real truth" were no longer available. Without the conception of reality we could not think of our knowledge in the fallibilistic mode we actually use—as having provisional, tentative, improvable features that constitute a crucial part of the conceptual scheme within whose orbit we operate our concept of inquiry.

Reality (in the traditional metaphysicians' construction of the concept) is the condition of things answering to "the real truth"; it is the realm of what really is as it really is. The pivotal contrast is between "mere appearance" and "reality as such," between "our picture of reality" and "reality itself," between what actually is and what we merely think (believe, suppose) to be. Our allegiance to the conception of reality, and to this contrast that pivots upon it, is rooted in the fallibilistic recognition that at the level of the detailed specifics of scientific theory, anything we presently hold to be the case may well turn out otherwise— indeed, will certainly do so if past experience gives any auguries for the future.

Our commitment to the mind-independent reality of "the real world" stands together with our acknowledgment that, in principle, any or all of our *present* scientific ideas as to how things work in the world, at *any* present, may well prove to be untenable. Our conviction in a reality that lies beyond our imperfect understanding of it (in all the various senses of "lying beyond") is rooted in our sense of the imperfections of our scientific world picture—its tentativity and potential fallibility. In abandoning our commitment to a mind-independent reality, we would lose the impetus of inquiry.

Sixth and finally, we need the conception of reality in order to operate the causal model of inquiry about the real world. Our standard picture of humanity's place in the scheme of things is predicated on the fundamental idea that there is a real world (however imperfectly our inquiry may characterize it) whose causal operations produce among other things causal impacts upon us, providing the basis of our world picture. Reality is viewed as the causal source and basis of the appearances, the originator and determiner of the phenomena of our cognitively relevant experience. "The real world" is seen as causally operative both in serving as the external moulder of thought and as constituting the ultimate arbiter of the adequacy of our theorizing. (Think here again of Peirce's "Harvard experiment.")

In summary, then, we need a postulate of an objective order of mind-independent reality for at least six important reasons:

1. To preserve the distinction between true and false with respect to factual matters and to operate the idea of truth as agreement with reality

2. To preserve the distinction between appearance and reality, between our *picture* of reality and reality itself

3. To serve as a basis for intersubjective communication

4. To furnish the basis for a shared project of communal inquiry

5. To provide for the fallibilistic view of human knowledge

6. To sustain the causal mode of learning and inquiry and to serve as a basis for the objectivity of experience

The conception of a mind-independent reality accordingly plays a central and indispensable role in our thinking with respect to matters of language and cognition. In communication and inquiry alike we seek to offer answers to our questions about how matters stand in this "objective realm." It is seen as the epistemological *object* of veridical cognition, in the context of the contrast between "the real" and its "merely phenomenal" appearances. Again, it is seen as the target of *telos* of the truth-estimation process at issue in inquiry, providing for a common focus in communication and communal inquiry. (The "real world" thus constitutes the "object" of our cognitive endeavors in both senses of this term—the *objective* at which they are directed and the *purpose* for which they are exerted.) Furthermore, reality is seen as the ontological *source* of cognitive endeavors, affording the existential matrix in which we move and have our being, and whose impact upon us is the prime mover for our cognitive efforts. All of these facets of the concept of reality are integrated and unified in the classical doctrine of truth as it corresponds to fact *(adaequatio ad rem),* a doctrine that only makes sense in the setting of a commitment to mind-independent reality.

Accordingly, the justification for this fundamental presupposition of objectivity is not *evidential* at all; postulates are not based on evidence. Rather, it is *functional.* We need this postulate to operate our conceptual scheme. The justification of this postulate lies in its utility. We could not form our existing conceptions of truth, fact, inquiry, and communication without presupposing the independent reality of an external world. We simply could not think of experience and inquiry as we do. (What we have here is a "transcendental argument" of sorts from the character of our conceptual scheme to the acceptability of its inherent presuppositions.) The primary validation of that crucial objectivity postulate lies in its basic functional utility in relation to our cognitive aims. It is worthwhile to explore more fully the implications of this circumstance.

Our commitment to an objective reality that lies behind the data that people secure is indispensably demanded by any step into that domain of publicly accessible objects that are essential to communal inquiry and interpersonal communication about a shared world. We do, and must, adopt a standard policy that prevails over all communicative discourse of letting the language we use—rather than whatever specific informative aims we may actually have in mind on particular occasions—be the decisive factor with regard to the things at issue in our discourse. For if we were to set up our own conception of things as somehow definitive and decisive, we would at once erect a barrier not only to further inquiry but also, and no less important, to the prospect of successful communication with one another. Communication requires not only common *concepts* but common *topics*, interpersonally shared items of discussion, a common world constituted by the self-subsistently real objects basic to shared experience. The factor of objectivity reflects our basic commitment to a communally available world as the common property of communicators. Such a commitment involves more than merely de facto intersubjective agreement. Such agreement is a matter of a posteriori discovery, whereas our view of the nature of things puts "the real world" on a necessary and a priori basis. This stance is rooted in the fundamental convention of a shared social instance of communication. What links my discourse with that of my interlocutor is our common subscription to the governing presumption (a defensible presumption, to be sure) that we are both talking about the shared thing, our own possible misconceptions of it notwithstanding. This means that no matter how extensively we may change our minds about the *nature* of a thing or type of thing, we are still dealing with exactly the same thing or sort of thing. It assures reidentification across discordant theories and belief systems.

An important lesson thus emerges. The rationale of a commitment to ontological objectivity is in the final analysis cognitively driven. Without a presuppositional commitment to objectivity with its acceptance of a real world independent of ourselves that we share in common, interpersonal communication would become impracticable. Objectivity is an integral part of the sine qua non presuppositional basis of the project of meaningful communication. To reemphasize, if our own subjective conceptions of things were to be determinative, informative communication about a world of shared objects and processes would be rendered unachievable.

Our concept of a *real thing* is such that it provides a fixed point, a stable center around which communication revolves, an invariant focus of potentially diverse conceptions. What is to be determinative, decisive, definitive of the things at issue in my discourse is not my conception, or yours, or indeed anyone's conception at all. The conventionalized intention discussed means that a coordination of conceptions is not decisive for the possibility of communication. Your statements about a thing may well convey something to me even if my conception of it is altogether different from yours. To communicate we need not take ourselves to share views of the world but only take the stance that we share the world being discussed. This commitment to an objective reality that underlies the data at hand is indispensably demanded by any step into the domain of the publicly accessible objects essential to communal inquiry and interpersonal communication about a shared world. We could not establish communicative contact about a common objective item of discussion if our discourse were geared to the substance of our own idiosyncratic ideas and conceptions.

3. The Idealistic Aspect of Metaphysical Realism

Realism is thus a position to which we are constrained not by the push of evidence but by the pull of purpose. Initially, at any rate, a commitment to realism is an *input* into our investigation of nature rather than an *output* thereof. At bottom, it does not represent a discovered fact but a methodological presupposition of our praxis of inquiry; its status is not constitutive (fact descriptive) but regulative (praxis facilitating). Realism is not a factual discovery but a practical postulate justified by its utility or serviceability in the context of our aims and purposes, seeing that if we did not *take* our experience to serve as an indication of facts about an objective order we would not be able to validate any objective claims whatsoever. (To be sure, what we can, and do, ultimately discover is that by taking this realistic stance we are able to develop a praxis of inquiry and communication that proves effective in the conduct of our affairs.)

The ontological thesis that there is a mind-independent physical reality to which our inquiries address themselves more or less adequately—and always imperfectly—is the key contention of realism and is supported by the deliberations set out earlier. But on the telling of the presenting analysis, this basic thesis has the epistemic status of a presuppositional postulate that is initially validated by its pragmatic utility and ultimately retrovalidated by the satisfactory results of its implementation (in both practical and theoretical respects). Our commitment to realism is, on this account, initially not a product of our *inquiries* about the world but rather reflects a facet of how we *conceive* the world. The sort of realism contemplated here is accordingly one that pivots on the fact that we *think* of real in a certain sort of way, and that in fact the very conception of the real is something we employ because doing so merits our ends and purposes.

Now insofar as realism ultimately rests on this pragmatic basis, it is not based on considerations of independent substantiating evidence about how things actually stand in the world but rather on considering, as a matter of practical reasoning, how we do (and must) think about the world within the context of the projects to which we stand committed. In this way, the commitment to a mind-independent reality plays an essentially utilitarian role as providing a functional requisite for our intellectual resources (specifically for our conceptual scheme in relation to communication and inquiry). Realism thus harks back to the salient contention of classical idealism that values and purposes play a pivotal role in our understanding of the nature of things. We return also to the characteristic theme of idealism—the active role of the knower not only in the constituting but also in the constitution of what is known.

To be sure, this sort of idealism is not substantive but methodological. It is not a rejection of real objects that exist independently of mind and as such are causally responsible for our objective experience; quite the reverse, it is designed to facilitate their acceptance. But it insists that the *rationale* for this acceptance lies in a framework of mind-supplied purpose. Our commitment to a mind-independent reality is seen to arise not *from* experience but *for* it—for the sake of putting us into a position to exploit our experience as a basis for validating inquiry and communication about the objectively real.

"Reality as such" is no doubt independent of our beliefs and desires, but what can alone concern us is reality as we view it. However, the only view of reality that is available to us is one that is devised by us under the aegis of principles of acceptability that we subscribe to because doing so serves our purposes. A position of this sort is in business as a realism all right. But given that it pivots on the character of our concepts and their modus operandi, it transpires that the business premises it occupies are actually mortgaged to idealism. The fact that objectivity is the fruit of communicative purpose allows idealism to infiltrate into the realist's domain.

The idealism at issue here cuts deeper yet. No doubt, we are firmly and irrevocably committed to the idea there is a physical realm out there that all scientific inquirers inhabit and examine alike. We hold to a single, uniform physical reality, insisting that all investigations exist within and investigate *it*: this single, shared realism, this single manifold of physical objects and laws. But this very idea of a single, uniform domain of physical object and laws represents just exactly that—*an idea of ours*. The idea is itself a matter of how we find it convenient and efficient to think about things: it is no more—though also no less—than the projection of a theory devised to sort the needs and conveniences of our intellectual situation. This approach endorses an object-level realism that rests on a presuppositional idealism at the justificatory infralevel. We arrive, paradoxical as it may seem, at a realism that is founded, initially at least, on a fundamentally idealistic basis—a realism whose ultimate *justificatory basis* is ideal.

Authentic realism can only exist in a state of tension. The only reality worth having is one that is to some degree knowable. But it is the very limitation of our knowledge—our recognition that there is more to reality than what we do and can know or ever conjecture about it—that speaks for the mind-independence of the real. It is important to stress against the skeptic that the human mind is sufficiently well attuned to reality that *some* knowledge of it is possible. But it is no less important to join with realists in stressing the independent character of reality, acknowledging that reality has a depth and complexity of makeup that outruns the reach of mind. This lesson is clearly brought home to us when we consider the inevitably processual and developmental aspect of our factual knowledge.

CHAPTER SEVEN

Process Philosophy and Historicist Relativism

1. Stage Setting: Historicity

Process philosophy represents an approach to philosophical issues that is of substantial interest and value in its own right. However, it also possesses substantial *instrumental* value. In particular, it is of great utility for the clarification and resolution of some philosophical problems that do not overtly lie in its own characteristic domain. An instructive illustration of this fact is provided by the much debated issue of historical relativism.

Unquestionably, everything that we humans manage to do is accomplished within a setting of place and time. The historical process envelops all our activities and dealings. Everything we do and undergo is a part of history, caught up in the grand macroprocess of human development and finding our due place in some local microcontext of era and culture. In thinking as in looking we can only view things from where we are. There is, for us, no Archimedean fulcrum outside the spatiotemporal historicity of place and era on which to pivot the lever of thought. As philosophers repeatedly insist, we have no possibility of achieving a "God's-eye view" or a "view from nowhere." Our activities—physical and mental alike—are inevitably part of the grand historical process, subject to the relativization of era and culture. The inexorable contextuality of things inescapably tethers our thought and action to our spatiotemporal placement in era and culture even as it ties our shadows to our physical placement on the earth's surface. We are trapped within history.

All of this is central to a historicist view of the world. And it deserves to be taken as a given, a fact of life, a straightforward statement of the way things are. This aspect of historical relativity must be acknowledged as undebatable and virtually truistic. What *is* debatable is just what follows from it. Given that human existence is unavoidably subject to historical conditions, just what inference can we properly make?

2. Cognitive Relativism

The main conclusion that is commonly drawn from the fact of historicity is epistemic relativism. The line of thought at issue here runs as follows: Theoreticians insist that the real truth of things is timeless and placeless—that what is indeed true is so always and everywhere. But human thought and belief are always historical, always issuing from and based in a setting of era and culture. This means that we have no way to determine what actually is true but only what people in certain places and times *think* to be such. Everything that we assert and accept is accompanied by the ubiquitous Kantian *I think*. We only have and can only ever achieve opinion and *putative* truth; the real article—the truth as such—lies outside our grasp. Belief and thought in general are always history-bound, whereas the real truth as such (if such there is) will be something that transcends history and thereby can reach us as well. The unavoidable conclusion here is that we cannot appropriately lay claim to securing the truth as such. We cannot escape historicity: if authentic and thereby timeless and placeless truth is where we want to go, then we have no way to get there from here. So reason the historicist advocates of cognitive relativism. Their argumentation is tempting—but at the same time profoundly fallacious.

3. The Perspective of Process

There is good reason to think that the fatal flaw of such a cognitive relativism lies in its failure to give due heed to the dialectic of process and product—and, in particular, the distinction between instances of the production of information and the items of information that are produced. Granted, thinking, inquiry, assertion, and the like are all intellectual processes carried on by humans that, as such, must inevitably have a historical setting by way of place and time, of culture and era. But this is clearly not the end of the matter. The reality of it is that there is no reason to think that changing historical process cannot reach out to changeless patterns of stability. The nearer we get to communicative basics, the more stable the result. Nothing about the historicity of our cognitive proceedings blocks the way to recognizing such timeless facts as that cats give birth to kittens, not woodchucks, and that oxygen bonds with hydrogen to make water, not alcohol. The *recognition* of such facts is unquestionably a matter of place and time, but this does not hold for these fact themselves.

The very idea of a process involves transtemporal constancies. Water evaporates. That is to say, the evaporation of water is a generic process; it has many instances, occurring alike after rainstorms in sixteenth-century Lima and in twentieth-century Atlanta. Any and every particular process is always an instantiation of a general pattern. One simply cannot identify a process that fails to be of a (processual) *type* and that, in consequence, is not, at that level of abstraction, capable of repetition. And so the concreta of history, viewed in an epistemic perspective, can in fact manage to transcend their space-time settings to instantiate general patterns. Although their manifestations are inevitably temporal and concrete, those processes themselves can be atemporal and generic.

Different concrete instances of a process can, of course, produce products of exactly the same generic type. Different factories can and often do produce the same model of car, and different cooks can and do produce the same variety of soup. This is strikingly so when the product happens to be information: different presses can print the same text, different respondents can give the same answer to the same question, different mouths can utter the same sentence, different minds can entertain the same idea.

The point is that in the realm of informational abstractness products can escape the limitations of their (invariably relativized) productive origins. The historical relativization of the production *process* to a particular historicocultural context—the fact that the thinking or the assertion of a truth is so relativized—in itself does nothing to limit the *product* (the truth that is so thought or asserted) to a historicocultural context. Once produced, it is generally available—and (insofar as abstract) will be cross-temporally accessible through its exemplifications and manifestations at different times and places. A currently fashionable position takes the following line:

> Different individuals and different societies live in altogether different thought worlds. We contemporary Westerners live in a realm of physical and chemical causation. Our primitive ancestors three millennia ago lived in an animistic realm of nature-spirit-wind gods, cloud spirits, and the like. There is no way to cross such conceptual divides. Every culture is entrapped in its own concept realm. The prospect of actual communication is unrealizable here. In consequence, since there is no way to effect contact, there is no prospect of any agreement or disagreement. As in matters of thought, so also in matters of action. Here there is no objective right or wrong either. To each his own—and to each his own is right and anything else altogether fallacious.

The fatal flaw of such a position is that it overlooks what might be characterized as the *unavoidable overlap* between any two conceptual realms that encompass a complexity sufficient to deal with "the real world."

Consider, for example, the well-known duck/rabbit drawing. You are schooled to see it as a duck, and I to see it as a rabbit, and never the two shall meet. Wrong! At the duck/rabbit level of conceptual complexity we indeed cannot come together. But when it comes down to more rudimentary talk about "a linear configuration that looks like *that* [pointing]," we are in coordination. You think of that object as a pencil, whereas I (who know nothing about such writing implements) think of it as a hairpin. Conceptually, we are miles apart. But both of us can agree that it is "a small wooden stick with a black something that comes to a point." I think the voodoo maven cast an evil spell on my neighbor; you think that this individual suffered through imaginative autosuggestion when he learned about the doll with its pin. Again, we are miles apart regarding how we think about the events at issue. But we have no trouble agreeing that "the maven stuck a pin through the head of the doll she used to represent the neighbor and he suffered illness as a somehow-produced result."

The point is that any complex concept scheme has internal resources through which the materials of another can be captured in a descriptively more rudimentary—and thereby descriptively neutral—manner so as to make communicative contact possible. Whatever is represented in the one can be represented in the other at a greater level of abstractness, but yet in sufficient detail to make communicative contact possible. There is never an absolutely unbridgeable gap, a total disconnection of conception. Anything can be characterized at a level sufficiently rudimentary to possibilize its accessibility to another scheme *at that level*. Your language may distinguish a hundred sorts of camels and twenty sorts of camel gaits, but your "Your camel is now gaiting" can be rendered in camel-naïve English as "Your camel is now moving in one of the fastest camel-characteristic modes"—a rendering that, notwithstanding its loss of information, helpfully approximates what is being said.

In this regard, the machinery of supposition, assumption, and hypothesis provide an absolutely crucial resource. Granted, we cannot *translate* the concept machinery of the Galenic humors into that of modern medicine. But this inability does not render the concept unavailable to the moderns. We can say, on the one hand, "Let's make an assumption. Suppose the heart were a furnace-type heat source, and that through its heating the blood warmth could be supplied to an animal's extremities. Then . . ." That is, we could unfold a story within a framework of assumptions that rendered the whole Galenic instrumentarium accessible to the modern mind. On the other hand, we could not *explain* modern medicine to the Galenic physician within the concept machinery of his favored theory. But we could certainly go back and *teach* it to him beginning with much the same presystematic conceptual resources that we use in bringing the modern student-novice into the realm of modern scientific medicine.

Thus, it may transpire that large-scale concept schemes used by different cultures can be so "disjointed" that one cannot be *translated* into the other. But they are never so disjointed that sufficient expository materials cannot be found within the resources of each to render the claims of the other accessible at a level of generality that allows an information transfer, which, however imperfect, suffices to make communicative contact possible. The problem is that the contemporary discussion of these issues only envisions extreme options: either total concept incommensurability or all-out concept identity. The intermediate situation that allows for a degree of concept consideration sufficient to provide for communicative contact is simply ignored. Yet it is just exactly here that the realities of the situation lie.

Accordingly, the inevitable historicity of all human proceedings does nothing to show that various beliefs and behaviors cannot be more than the characteristic possession of a transient and temporary era in the history of a particular culture. The processual aspect of human thought provides the basis for its capacity to rise above its episodic particularities.

4. Transcending Origins: Escaping Historicity through Information

Two concessions must be granted to the relativist: (1) different bodies of evidence will be available in the varying circumstances of different times and places (in the wake, for example, of archeological research or of document discoveries), and (2) different frameworks for interpreting available evidence will come to light (such as in the course of medical or psychological research). Clearly, such changes in the volume or bearing of the evidence will change our views about what the truth of the matter is. But these changes, of course, affect just that—our views. They do not alter the facts of the matter. If we should learn that Caesar had an egg for breakfast on that fateful day in March, this discovery would relate to a change in our information about the thing but would not effect a change in Caesar himself from a non-egg breakfaster to an egg breakfaster. The "change" occurring when Caesar shifts from being a person thought of *X*-wise to one thought of *Y*-wise is no real change *in Caesar* at all but rather a change in the state of thinking about him.

Information, in particular, is a special sort of product—one that is inherently abstract. There is the actual making or staking of a claim (which is always biographical and therefore historical) and the claim that is made, which exists ahistorically outside of space and time. The factor of abstraction means that we must distinguish the believing from the belief; the theorizing from the theory; the assuming from the assumption. Different people at different times and places have the same beliefs, project the same theories, and make the same assumptions. The history-bound nature of the concrete episode (the believing, theorizing, assuming) does not affect the ahistorical nature of the informative item at issue (the belief, theory, assumption). Those concrete particulars that we perceive or contemplate may be specific particulars, but the thought instrumentalities we employ represent generic processes. Think of the color green versus green things (a leaf, a lawn), or the number two versus pairs of things (twins, ears). To historicize them is to treat them as concrete things and thereby to commit the fallacy of misplaced concreteness, as Whitehead called it.

Bearing in mind the distinction between the transhistorical (omni-temporal) and the ahistorical (timeless) is important here. Genuine laws of nature (fundamental physical laws) are omnitemporal: they hold always and everywhere—they pervade space-time, so to speak. But purely abstract conditional relationships—conditional if-then connections, for example—are atemporal. (Vertebrates and canines are historical entities, but conceptual facts on the order of "if something is a canine, then it is a vertebrate" are, by nature, timeless and ahistorical, holding always and everywhere, even when canines and vertebrates are absent.) The abstractness of information is something that, by its very nature, carries us outside the scheme of history. In other words, though the *learning* or *imparting* of information is always historical, the information that we learn or impart need not be. Cognitive and communicative processes are indeed spatiotemporal, but the objects they involve can be abstract. And this has a significant bearing upon our present concerns.

Some sorts of things exist out of space but not out of time—for example, one's ownership of a piece of jewelry and one's right to exercise an option to purchase a tract of land. Other sorts of things exist neither in space nor in time—numbers, facts, and generalized relationships, for example. (The Eiffel Tower was erected in Paris in the nineteenth century, but the fact that Julius Caesar did not realize this is something that has no spatiotemporal emplacement.) Information is like that. The things that information may be about may be spatiotemporal, as will be the speech or writing by which the information is conveyed from one person to another. But the information itself is altogether nonspatiotemporal. It simply lies in the nature of certain sorts of things, information included, not to be located in space and time but to be "abstract."

Admittedly, when we are viewing something, the only views we can possibly obtain are views from somewhere (and from viewpoints belonging to us and not to God). But when the viewing is done with the eyes of the mind, and its object is the realm of information rather than the realm of physical reality, then what the view is a view of is something ahistorical. Information as such exists outside of history even though our acquiring it is invariably a historical transaction. We must avert the category mistake of confusing process with product here: of conflating the information that we access with the historical actions and events of our accessing it.

Of course, we have no way to get to the abstract (the belief) except through the historical (the believing). But what we achieve (the product) is something of a nature different and status distinct from the mode of its realization (the process). When we engage ourselves in intellectual processes that carry us into the informational domain, we impel ourselves from history into an ahistorical sphere. The same idea (the same thought process, the same belief) is accessible to people at different times and places. Were it not so, communication would be altogether impossible.

The overall situation in matters of abstraction is triadic (to use the term favored by Peirce). There are (1) the various and sundry concrete green things, (2) the abstract property at issue (namely, the property or characteristic of being green), and (3) the mediative conception or idea of greenness that is the thought instrumentability through which that abstract property comes to be imputed to those concrete items that putatively manifest it. The medieval metaphysical dispute between nominalism, conceptualism, and platonism needs to be resolved *conjunctively*. All three are needed: a nominalism is required for particulars, a conceptualism is required for concepts, and a platonism is required for abstractions. The situation is not one of either/or; we must endorse all those doctrinal positions, each in its own place. After all, were it not for generic processes that reach across the limits of space and time, those nominalistic commonalties would not, could not be there.

Yet how can temporalized thought deal in timeless information? How is it that particularized episodic thought can make episode-abstractive generalizations? The long and short of it is that thought just works that way. To puzzle about this is like puzzling about how it is that money can be used to buy things or that words can be used for speaking. Once the world's brute realities have been taken in stride, the problem is left behind.

Fundamental problems—such as how standardized exchange and verbal communication are possible—lie in the background here. But once such fundamental issues are resolved, the original question is dissolved as such: something that is not a medium of exchange would not be called money, nor would something that could not play a generalized role in verbal or written communication be called a word. Even so, something would not be called thought if it could not function abstractly to convey general information transcending the episodic occurrences at issue.

5. Against a Monistic Nominalism of Concreta

To make a success of the idea of being "trapped within history" we would need to be nominalistic extremists who project an ontology of concreta alone, denying the conceptualists' idea that abstractions can be manifested through such concreta in a way that enables them to achieve generality. The circumstance that concreta can instantiate or exemplify transcending generalities would have to be abandoned. But taking a process point of view indicates that this is eminently unrealistic. Clearly, the atemporalities and transtemporalities of nature's processes can be exemplified in the world's experienced concreta that "participate" (to use Plato's term) in them.

Human action and experience embed us in the order of concrete reality within a particularized setting of spatiotemporal and causal order. But ideas and information carry us into a universal (abstract) order that our experiential concreteness *instantiates* but does not *encompass*. Intelligence, with its characteristically mental processes, provides for a linkage that mediates between these two realms. It lies in the very nature of intelligent beings to function as "amphibians" able by fusing percepts and concepts to operate conjointly and concurrently in the realms of both concrete experience and abstract thought.

In the domain of *bodily* action we are indeed trapped within history, but *intellectual* action provides us with an escape—a means of entering the region of abstract generality. Intelligence is able to effect the transit from the episodically causal (the thinking) to the abstractly rational (the thought)—and, in matters of discourse, from the concrete declaring to the generic declaration. All such intellectual processes involve the projection from spatiotemporal specificity to informative generality. With thought—unlike bodily action—we can move beyond the present into the past and future and indeed from the realm of the real into that of the merely possible. Present action can only replicate but not actually repeat past actions, whereas present thoughts can not only replicate but even repeat past thoughts. Intelligent agents operate both in the realm of the causality of nature and the realm of the causality of reason. For them, experiences such as "cat-on-mat sighting" have a double aspect, able at once to engender and (in view of imprinted practical policies) to justify suitable beliefs that have a generalized bearing. Accordingly, such intelligent agents are able to have dual-function experiences that at once cause their beliefs and provide the reasons for holding them.

6. Causality and Comprehension

The embedding of occurrences in the order of causality is conditioned by context and unrepeatable. But this is not so in the order of comprehension. In reaching the realm of abstractions, thought and comprehension cut their objects of concern loose from their experiential moorings.

With intelligent creatures, then, causality and comprehension become conjoined. The "conscious experience of taking oneself to have a cat perception of a suitable sort"—exactly because it is a cognitively significant experience—at once and concurrently constitutes the *cause* of X's claiming that "the cat is on the mat" and affords X with a *reason* for making this claim. In the cognitive experience of intelligent beings, there are not separate domains of causes and of reasons: here the occurrence of one and the same experience can at once constitute both the cause of and the reason for a belief exactly because that is the sort of "experience" that is at issue.

Intelligent agency brings something new upon nature's scene in the course of its own functioning. Consider the following exchange:

> "What causally produced his belief that the cat is on the mat?"
> "He saw it there."
> "Why—for what reason—does he claim that the cat is on the mat?"
> "He saw it there."

His seeing experience is a matter of dual action in both modes of causality. Certain sorts of eventuations are "amphibious" because they operate at once and concurrently *both* in the realm of natural causes *and* in the realm of reasons. My perspective experience of "seeing the cat on the mat" is at once the cause of my belief and affords my reason for holding that belief. With intelligent agents such as ourselves, conscious *experiences* do double duty as eventuations in nature and as reasons for belief.

For intelligent beings whose modi operandi are suitably shaped by their evolutionary heritage, the step from experience to belief is at once causal *and* rational: we hold the belief *because* of the experience both in the order of efficient *and* in the order of final (rational) causation. With intelligent creatures such as ourselves, experiences of certain sorts are dual-purpose; their occurrence both causally engenders and rationally justifies the holding of certain beliefs. Informatively meaningful perceptions and physical stimuli run together in unison. One recent writer declares: "But while the actual occurrence of happiness or unhappiness, pleasure or pain, etc., is indeed beyond our control . . . the same does not seem obviously to hold for our beliefs about such matters. . . . These beliefs or judgments . . . can . . . be arbitrarily manipulated at will, so long as the other elements are appropriately adjusted."[1] It would thus be contended, for example, that while the *actual occurrence* of pain, suffering, or disappointment may be extratheoretical, nevertheless a person's *awareness* of such things is not, since awareness lies only in the area of belief, of mere opinion. Having the experience and coming to the belief—actually *having* the pain and *thinking* that one does—can thus be altogether detached from one another. But this way of regarding the matter is flawed because its assumption of separability is deeply problematic.

The fact is that beliefs are concurrently produced *and* justified by experiences. My belief that the cat is on the mat need not rest on the further and different *belief* that I see it there; it can rest directly and immediately on my experience of seeing it. In other words, beliefs do not always require a justification through other beliefs but can rest directly on appropriate experiences. One's reason for holding a belief need not be yet another belief but can simply be an experience—an experience that *produces* (from a causal point of view) and *validates* and *justifies* (from a probative point of view) that belief.

7. Communicative Processes

The dual nature of personal experience lies at the root of interpersonal communication; for it is exactly this, the coordination of concrete causes and abstract beliefs, that underwrites the shift from particular experiences to universal ideas. Communication is by nature a process of conveying information. And information, in turn, is by its very nature something general and abstract. If you are to understand me when I talk about apples, then the words I use must find purchase in the realm of your experience as well as mine. Information transfer could not take place between us if our terms of reference were wholly disconnected. This means that the instrumentalities by which the process of communication works must transcend the limits of their concrete historical foothold in this order of space and time. We must be prepared to view them under the aegis of a shared generality.

In matters of communication, subscription to an objective reality—one that, as such, is abstractly independent of the historical vagaries of individualized discussion episodes—is something indispensably demanded by any step into the domain of the publicly accessible objects essential to communal inquiry and interpersonal communication about a shared world. We could not establish communicative contact with one another regarding a common objective item of discussion if our discourse related solely to our own activities and our personalized conceptions that are bound up with them. The conventionalized intention to take impersonal objects to be at issue is fundamental because it is overriding—that is, it overrides all of our other intentions when we enter the communicative venture. Without this communally conventionalized intention we should not be able to convey information—or misinformation—to one another about a shared "objective" world that underlies and connects those historical discourse activities of ours.

It is thus crucial to the communicative enterprise to take an egocentrism-avoiding stance that rejects all claims to a privileged status for *our own* conception of things as bound to our own particular historical position in the world's processual scheme. If our communicative mechanisms were inseparably confined to the concrete conditions of their use—to the particular space and time and range of concern of their employment—communication would become impracticable. One could then never advance the issue of communicative focus upon a single item of mutual concern beyond the status of a more or less well-grounded *assumption* so that communication would no longer be an exchange of information but a tissue of frail conjectures. Only by using the resources of thought to free our conceptual resources from the concrete spatiotemporal context of their employment can we manage to communicate with one another across the reaches of space and time. Only by subscribing to a fundamental reality postulate regarding objective things and ideas that transcend the limits of our own cognitive reach can we implement the sort of view of experience, inquiry, and communication that we in fact have. Without this, the entire conceptual framework of our thinking about the world and our place within it would come crashing down.

The viability of abstraction as a process that transcends the limits of context thus follows by a transcendental argument from the possibility of communication to the "conditions under which alone" communication is possible. Thus, to the extent that Cicero's contemporaries could gain access to his thoughts through his deeds and his writings, so, in principle, can we. Communication and information transfer can take place only to the extent that we can reach beyond the historical concreta of our experience and function at a level of processive abstraction.

A concretizing particularism of the nominalistic sort ("there are no abstracta") is totally at odds with process philosophy's commitment to cognitive and communicative processes. A concrete process is always an instantiation of a general process type. It is axiomatic in process philosophy that "to be a process is to be a process of a certain specifiable sort." In the setting of a process theory of mind, this fundamental fact carries us from sporadic cognitive experiences to the abstractions required to underwrite the possibility of communication and information management.

* * *

The idea that we can be cognitively trapped within history by a relativism that tethers us to our context of time and culture founders on fundamental considerations of process thought—and, in particular, on the role of information in the communicative process. When evolution produces an intelligent social being on the order of *Homo sapiens*, it thereby brings into existence a creature equipped with the intellectual resources to enter into the communicative realm in a way that enables it to transcend the historical concreteness of its particular spatiotemporal context of existence. By virtue of being the kind of thing it is, such a creature is no longer "trapped within history." Indeed, if we were so trapped in the way that doctrinaire epistemic relativism insists upon, then any and all prospects of communication across the divide of space and time would be annihilated. To take such a position would be to deny one of the most fundamental realities of the human condition—that we are living, breathing creatures rooted in the processual setting of a communicative community.[2]

CHAPTER EIGHT

Process Philosophy and Monadological Metaphysics

1. Monads and the Identity of Indiscernibles

Monadological metaphysics is intimately bound to process philosophy; from the days of Leibniz and Boscovitch, process-oriented thinking has figured prominently in monadological philosophizing.

The term *monad* is used in both a physical and a metaphysical sense. Physically, monads are centers of force or activity—loci characterized by a dynamic impetus to change. Metaphysically, monads are existing items (units of reality) whose identities lie in their descriptive uniqueness. One of the prime objectives of this discussion is to show how these two seemingly discordant features are interrelated.

A pivotal contention of monadological metaphysics is that concrete particulars (individuals, objects, items) can be individuated or identified descriptively. Monadology stands committed to the idea that anything concrete admits of a specific identifying description. The doctrine thus pivots on a distinctive approach to ontological item identification. Its maxim is: To be as a unit of existence is to be uniquely characterizable. And so the pivotal question arises: What assumptions must one make about a "world" (i.e., an existential manifold) if its individuals are to be identifiable by purely descriptive means? What can be said about the nature of a world whose concrete constituents exhibit descriptive uniqueness?

In the interest of clarifying these issues, let F be the set of the various descriptive features that the objects of consideration can possibly exhibit, and let f be a variable that ranges over these features. Moreover, let $X, Y, Z, \ldots$ be the objects of consideration; and let DX, the complete description of object X, be the subset of F containing all of those features that are exhibited by X. Thus,

$$DX = \{f : fX\}.$$

The answer to our focal question may now be indicated schematically as follows: A world whose individuals admit of descriptive identification must be such that each of its members has its own characteristic and uniquely identifying description, so that

$$DX = DY \text{ iff } X = Y.$$

Stated differently, this comes down to

$$X = Y \text{ iff } \forall f(fX \equiv fY).$$

Accordingly, the world in question is one in which the principle of the identity of (descriptive) indiscernibles obtains. In a monadology, to be is to be the bearer of a unique descriptive identity. This principle of descriptive individuation lies at the very core of a monadological ontology.

2. Identification by Ostension and Space-Time Positioning

It must be acknowledged from the start that such a monadology is not inevitable: alternative approaches to metaphysics can certainly be developed on the basis of different modes of individuation. In particular, to identify (individuate) an object within this actual world of ours, we do not require complete descriptions—incomplete descriptions will do. Consider, for example, "that apple tree [pointing]" and "that cat on yonder mat [pointing]." As such examples indicate, objects can also be identified ostensively by pointing or using some other suitable gesture. And this process of ostension, of pointing or otherwise physically indicating, can shrink description to an irreducible minimum in matters of identification. (Presumably it can never be reduced to zero. If I simply say "that" and point, there will always be alternatives: the apple, say, or its skin or its color.)

Reliance on ostension, however, has obvious drawbacks. It depends crucially upon a relationship of juxtaposition among a confronting identifier, a confronted object, and whoever happens to be the beneficiary of the identification. All three have to be duly co-located for the ostensive identification to be practicable. The need for this fortuitous factor of co-presence means that this identifactory process suffers from severe limitations. For one thing, for us, ostension is limited to our world and to our locale within it. Moreover, although we can offer descriptions to our distant posterity, we cannot point things out to them. Nor can future objects or nonphysical objects, such as poems, or abstract objects, such as rights, ever be identified ostensively.

To be sure, ostensive indication can in many cases be exchanged for emplacement in a coordinate system. When something is positioned within a preexisting or pre-given space-time framework, one can again proceed with object identification on the basis of partial and very complete descriptions; for example, the apple trees growing in such-and-such a place at a certain time, and the cat on the mat located in a certain place at a certain time. Since distinct physical objects are spatiotemporally exclusive of one another, they can be identified with minimal descriptions within a given space-time framework in this sort of coordinate-indicative way. But a big problem nevertheless remains, for coordinates are never cognitively self-sufficient. To make effective use of coordinates, *we need to determine just where those coordinates themselves are positioned.* They must be identified by place markers that themselves will ultimately require ostensive identification. Coordinates thus reduce the need for ostension, but they cannot entirely remove it. As long as ostension is necessary for the identification of individuals, we do not have the requisite conditions or an adequate ontology.

3. An Impetus to Monadology

But why should one envision a monadological approach here? Why not rest satisfied with individuating particulars by means of an ostension-requiring spatiotemporal placement—supplemented by partial descriptions as needed?

The reasons for discontent are clear if one is a Leibnizian space-time relativist who thinks that individuals have an identity that is logically antecedent to any positioning within a spatiotemporal framework and that space-time itself arises emergently through the concrete individuals that, commonly speaking, "occupy it." Again, the grounds for discontent are also clear if one accepts a theology of creation *ex nihilo* that calls for a conceptualized individuation of the world's contents "antecedently" to the realization of any spatiotemporal manifold in which these items are actualized. Moreover, they are also clear if one subscribes to a conceptualistic ontology with respect to possibilia, holding the view that for possibles, "to be is to be described" so that descriptive individuation is a requisite. Accordingly, there are many points of view requiring reliance on a monadological approach in metaphysics.

However, something deeper is also at work—a factor that, more than any other, supports a monadological approach. This is the desirability of an individuating mechanism that is at once general in its range and independent of issues of fortuitous placement—be it of ourselves, of the objects of our attention, or of the relationship between them. Leibniz's God had to identify things from a vantage point entirely *outside* the space-time framework. We ourselves need not go so far, but metaphysics can certainly ask for an identification process that is independent of (or invariant under) one's position *within* it. Now ostension, as indicated earlier, is an inherently imperfect and limited communicative device for purposes of identification since it depends on a fortuitous spatiotemporal relationship, resting on factors that are, to all appearances, accidental, transitory, and incidental to the item at issue—namely, on spatial relationships between an observer and the objects of the observer's interactions. This is clearly a disadvantage from the metaphysical point of view, given that a satisfactory metaphysic must avoid reliance upon ostension because such relationships are not inherent in the nature of the objects. It should acknowledge that identity must rest on certain features that are essential to an object—at least in the aggregate—and that spatiotemporal characteristics are always accidental. Only when objects are identified through features of their own nature (which thus prescind from incidental relations to their observing interagents) can an objectivistic metaphysics rest satisfied. Perhaps such a traditionalistic metaphysic is unrealizable—perhaps its demands cannot be met. But this is something that is far from clear—and, in any case, is a conclusion that we should reach only as a last resort.

4. Describing Individuals

But how can the individuation of objects proceed when one abstracts them altogether from their spatiotemporal positioning? Clearly, our only recourse at this point is to proceed by descriptive means alone. This means that we would have to provide a *complete* description of an object for identification to be assured, for as long as our descriptions remain incomplete, they can never securely fix upon a particular object. When there is any sort of incompleteness, there will always be a plurality of alternatives—that is, a variety of different (because *descriptively* different) possible realizations of individuals that otherwise correspond to that incomplete description. The uniqueness essential to identification would be lacking, just exactly because descriptive blanks can always be filled in in several different ways.

Even with complete descriptions, however, we are still not home free regarding identification. We also require the restrictivity of a law of nature that guarantees the exclusivity of uniqueness to "complete" descriptions. As noted earlier, purely descriptive individuation—identification that dispenses with any reliance upon positioning individuals in a space-time framework—is unproblematic only in worlds where a descriptive "exclusion principle" obtains. Only then will a principle of the identity of (descriptive) indiscernibles be in operation so that once one object occupies a particular descriptive "compartment" (so to speak), all others are excluded therefrom. But how can such a principle be validated? Clearly, we can accomplish this in one of two ways: (1) as a matter of logicoconceptual principle, which would require us to take a world-internal standpoint and allow relational predicate (being related in some X-wise rather than some Y-wise way) to play an identifactory role; or (2) as a matter of natural law, which would require us to see the world as de facto subject to a descriptive exclusion principle that provides the basis for a principle of the identity of indiscernibles (a theory of nature such as, after Leibniz, that space is emergent from or supervenient upon the individuals it contains would suffice to assure this). But in the first, relational, case we again rely on something fortuitous—namely, relational concatenation itself. Only the second, nomic, route will take us to the destination we seek. The exclusion law may itself be contingent, but being a law, it is at least not something fortuitous and idiosyncratic. It has a rationale, even when this rationale contains elements of fact. To be sure, Leibniz thought that we could assure descriptive individuation on logicoconceptual grounds alone subject to his understanding of space. But he could take this stance only because he operated his monadology from a world-external, God's-eye-view perspective. But this Leibnizian vantage point is not available to mere mortals.

5. The Turn to Process

The issue of descriptive individuation has another noteworthy aspect. For to have any chance of being effective, the descriptive approach to individual identification has to take into account the element of time. To see why this should be so, let us suppose a micromanifold of descriptive properties with just four members: two for shape (spherical and cubical) and two for color (red and green). Observe that on this basis we are able to arrive at just four (2 x 2) possible individual descriptions, namely *SR*, *SG*, *CR*, and *CG*. More generally, it is clear that a world which admits of only a limited number of descriptive properties, f_1, f_2, ... f_n (for the moment, let us suppose them to be of a binary on-or-off nature), will admit only a finite number of individual descriptions, namely, 2^n, because an individual has two possibilities, on and off, with respect to each f_i. The descriptive possibilities in any such world are therefore relative to the number of properties available. Here the fertility of concreta makes enormous demands on the complexity of the operative abstracta. The interests of theoretical economy and elegance are gravely compromised.

However, the situation changes radically when we invoke time with its correlatives change and process. For suppose that we proceed to temporalize properties. Then in place of "*X* has/lacks *f*," we have "*X* has/lacks *f* at time *t*." And on this basis we move straightaway to the dynamics of changing possession or degree of possession of properties over time. Thus even in a discrete time-framework, our prior example yields a vast manifold of descriptive possibilities: for color, *RGGGG* . . ., *RGRGRG* . . ., and so on; and for shape, *SSSSS* . . ., *CCSCCSCCS* . . ., and so on. When our descriptions become temporalized and thereby able to spell out processes of internal change and external interaction, they become vastly more prolific and powerful. On a temporal basis, descriptive uniqueness is no longer ontologically impoverishing when individuals become identified as loci of complex properties. The floodgate is thrown open to immense variation once the world is describable with temporal machinery—that is, with differential equations rather than the classic Aristotelian machinery of objects with merely qualitative rather than quantitative features. (Note that this processualism does not—or not as yet—involve a position in spacetime relative to other individuals, but is still a matter of the internal descriptive make-up of particulars.)

This line of thought leads to the central point. Comparatively speaking, the descriptive resources of atemporal properties are too impoverished to provide for a plausible "world" of descriptively individuated individuals and thereby unable to operate a successful monadology. But if one shifts to a quantitative perspective that adopts the parameterization of time and degree and thereby introduces a dynamic and processual perspective, it opens up the prospect of a greatly more plausible metaphysic. Accordingly, *if* one is going to develop a metaphysic monadologically through a principle of descriptive individuation, *then* the effective natural way to proceed is through a metaphysic of processes.

In conceptualizing monads in line with this perspective—as temporally unfolding successions of states that characterize an object's history—we are taking an effectively processual view of reality. A process, after all, is nothing other than a temporally structured manifold of spheres or stages. And time-indexing by itself is not enough here: we need to resort to temporally structured laws of development. And this is exactly how monads are best conceived of—namely, as so many unique instantiations or exemplifications of natural processes. It thus becomes clear that the idea of process affords the natural (and only sensible) approach to the development of a monadological metaphysic, with a monad's uniquely identifying overall description construed as a cluster of processes.

As is clear from this perspective, thinking of monads in processual terms rather than in substantial terms makes far more sense. A monad, so considered, is characterized by a pattern of activity—a macroprocess encompassing all of the microprocesses characteristic of the object's history. It is, for all intents and purposes, a process or a coordinated concatenation of processes. From such an ontological perspective, there is no stability to the world's things. Given the rich and complex world picture that is now secured, the only stable aspect will be the world's laws—its processes or lawful patterns of occurrence. Its substantival materials become phenomenal, immersed in a sea of process.

There are other good reasons for conceiving of monads in processive term rather than in terms based on the substance-property model. To be a substance, there must be an ongoingly self-identical bit of physical reality—a substantial core or essence—that assumes or discards properties over time. The paradigm of a core property bearer with variable properties is pivotal here. But just this sort of thing, a changeless core, is effectively impossible to come by in a world subject to pervasive and unremitting change in its substantial contents.

Of course, the change of properties over time can be either chaotic or orderly. Change can occur randomly or in discriminable patterns, governed by such rules as, "whenever a property configuration of type 1 is realized, a property configuration of type 2 will ensue." Such rules of processual regularity define dispositions. In an orderly world, substances will not only be temporally complex in terms of property variation but also temporally orderly, in that their property changes will manifest lawful dispositions. This situation, of course, is exactly what a *process* is all about. A monadology of descriptively identified individuals accordingly cries out for complex dynamicized properties. Monadological metaphysics issues an open invitation to a processual (dynamical) implementation. It is thus no wonder that Leibniz's theory took exactly this route.

6. Coda

In the end, then, our deliberations lead back to the theme of the opening paragraph. We there began by noting that monadology has two aspects: (1) a physical aspect in which monads are units of process—centers of force and activity, so to speak; and (2) a metaphysical aspect in which monads are units of concrete existence that admit of descriptive individuation. The line of thought developed here indicates that these two salient aspects of monadological metaphysics are coordinated. It indicates that the natural articulation of a descriptive metaphysics of particulars moves in the direction of seeing such items as both the manifestations of processes and the product of their natural unfolding.

NOTES

Chapter 1

1. A. N. Whitehead, *The Concept of Nature* (Cambridge: Cambridge University Press, 1920), chap. 3.

2. A. N. Whitehead, *Process and Reality* (Cambridge: Cambridge University Press, 1929), 47, 124.

3. Ibid., 318, 471.

4. The events that constitute a process must be temporally coordinated. But they need not be casually connected. The king's morning toilette is a process: he arises, and then washes, and then brushes his teeth, and so on. The unifying linkage of this complex process is "and then." But there is no connection (he does not brush his teeth *because* he has washed). Such examples show that specifically *causal* processes constitute only a particular sort of process.

5. Jean-Paul Sartre, "Bad Faith," in *Being and Nothingness,* trans. Hazel Barnes (New York: Pocket Books, 1966), 107–108.

6. David Hume, "Of Personal Identity," in *A Treatise of Human Nature,* bk. II, pt. IV, sec. 6. In the appendix, Hume further elaborates: "When I turn my reflection on *myself,* I never can perceive this *self* without some one or more perceptions; nor can I ever perceive anything but the perceptions. It is the composition of these, therefore, which forms the SELF."

7. Miguel de Unamuno, *Del sentimiento trágico de la vida,* ed. P. Felix Garcia (Madrid: Espasa-Calpe, 1976), 52.

8. For a useful anthology on the topic, see Ewert H. Cousins, ed., *Process Theology: Basic Writings* (New York: Newman Press, 1971), which seeks to integrate the tradition of Whitehead with that of Teilhard de Chardin.

9. Andrew J. Reck, "Process Philosophy: A Categorical Analysis" in *Studies in Process Philosophy II*, ed. R. C. Whattemore, Tulane Studies in Philosophy 24 (New Orleans: Tulane University, 1975), 59.

10. This draws on Nicholas Rescher, "Process Philosophy," in *Frontiers in American Philosophy*, ed. Robert W. Burch and Herman J. Saatkamp, Jr. (College Station, Tex.: Texas A&M University Press, 1992; reprint, as "On the Promise of Process Philosophy," *Process Studies* 25 [1996]:55–71). I am indebted to Johanna Seibt and David Carey for constructive comments on a draft of this discussion.

Chapter 2

1. William James, *The Principles of Psychology*, 2 vols. (New York: Henry Holt, 1890), 1:243.

2. This aspect of process was particularly stressed in George Herbert Mead's Carus lectures in *The Philosophy of the Present*, ed. A. E. Murphy (Chicago: University of Chicago Press, 1972).

3. For informative deliberations regarding the concept of process, see Donald Hanks, "Process as a Categorical Concept," in *Studies in Process Philosophy II*, ed. R. C. Whattemore, Tulane Studies in Philosophy 24 (New Orleans: Tulane University, 1975), 38–45.

4. G. W. F. Hegel, *Encyclopedia*, sec. 352, addendum.

5. A. N. Whitehead, *Process and Reality*, ed. D. R. Griffin and D. W. Sherbourne (New York: Macmillan, 1978), 30. "The real actual things that endure are all societies. They [namely, enduring things] are not actual occasions [which are always short-lived]." A. N. Whitehead, *Adventures of Ideas* (New York: Macmillan, 1933), 262. For Whitehead, both physical things (trees, tables, cats) and subatomic particles are "corpuscular societies." For a more thorough processist, they could all be seen as simply constellations of process.

6. C. S. Peirce, *Collected Papers,* vol. 6, ed. C. Hartshorne and P. Weiss (Cambridge, Mass: Harvard University Press, 1934), sec. 169, 170.

Chapter 3

1. W. V. Quine, *Word and Object* (Cambridge, Mass.: MIT Technology Press, 1960).

2. Nicholas Rescher, review of *Word and Object,* by W. V. Quine, *American Scientist* 48 (1960):375A-77A.

3. Nelson Goodman, *Structure of Appearance* (Cambridge Mass.: Harvard University Press, 1951).

4. Michael Dummett, "A Defense of McTaggart's Proof of the Unreality of Time, " *Philosophical Review* 69 (1960):497-504. However, Dummett's (and McTaggart's) discussion can be construed as being inimical to the "revolt against process" in that their support of the "unreality" of time may be viewed as an argument for its *sui generis* character and a protest against its assimilation to space.

5. Donald Williams, "The Myth of Passage," *Journal of Philosophy,* 48 (1951):457-72.

6. Richard Taylor, "Spatial and Temporal Analogies and the Concept of Identity," *Journal of Philosophy,* 52 (1955):599-612.

7. One of the few relevant discussions is found in Margaret Macdonald, "Things and Processes," *Analysis* 6 (1938):85-98, reprinted in *Philosophy and Analysis,* ed. M. Macdonald (New York: Philosophy Library, 1954). But this article avoids arduous effort by having an easy time of it with the extremist thesis: "There are no things but only processes." After all, even the most dedicated processist can make room for things as suitable constellations of processes.

8. D. S. Schwayder, *Modes of Referring and the Problem of Universals: An Essay in Metaphysics,* University of California Publications in Philosophy, vol. 35 (Berkeley, 1961).

9. P. F. Strawson, Individuals: An Essay in Descriptive Metaphysics (London: Methuen, 1959).

10. I use the term *ontological priority* here in its generic presystematic sense, rather than in Strawson's technical sense (p. 59), which renders tautological the thesis that material objects are ontologically prior in "our conceptual scheme."

11. The fact that numbers might not qualify as "particulars" in someone's conception is immaterial for this counterexample. Identification through some attached physical icon would serve our purpose just as well.

12. It is difficult to see how someone who purports to be a *descriptive* metaphysician can maintain the subordination of processes to things on the basis of ultimately linguistic considerations, considering that the "conceptual scheme" of our ordinary use of language puts things/nouns and processes/verbs pretty much on all fours with each other.

13. An influential paper by Wilfrid Sellars may also be mentioned in this connection. See Sellars, *Time and the World Order,* Minnesota Studies in the Philosophy of Science, vol. 3 (Minneapolis: University of Minnesota Press, 1962).

14. The preceding part of the chapter draws on Nicholas Rescher, "The Revolt against Process," *Journal of Philosophy* 59 (1962):410–17. The subsequent sections draw on Nicholas Rescher, "On Situating Process Philosophy," *Process Studies* 28 (1999):37–42.

15. Arthur O. Lovejoy, "The Thirteen Pragmatisms," *Journal of Philosophy, Psychology, and Scientific Methods* 5 (1908):5–12, 29–39.

Chapter 4

1. The *identification* of a citation is a matter infinitely simpler than its *description* because of the individuating role of spatiotemporal indicators. Both "that stroking of a beard" (pointing) and "Winterson's beard stroking just now" suffice fully to identify an action but do very little toward describing it. Identification can be virtually barren of descriptive detail.

2. Note that this is the fundamental item in the specification of an action, and that the "it" that occurs in the wording of all the other questions refers to the relevant instance of the act-type in question.

3. To identify a (concrete) action, it suffices to specify the agent, the act-type, and the occasion (time) of acting. But to say this is not, of course, to say that the adequate description of an action does not require a good deal more.

4. There are some striking similarities between the questions presented in the tabulation and those inherent in Aristotle's *Categories*. But explicit consideration of the matter would carry us too far afield.

5. The common parlance "to cause" and "to motivate" do not contrast neatly in the way philosophers would wish in order to draw the contrast. Compare the locutions "Her hesitancy caused him to persevere" or "My importunity caused him to reconsider the decision."

6. There are, of course, a great many others, for example, gladly/reluctantly and confidently/hesitantly.

7. As with items of behavior best not called actions, though in many ways related to them, such as reflex reactions or such "automatic" behavior as sneezing. In the interests of clarity such items, with respect to which the issues of finality and intentionality do not arise at all, should be excluded from the rubric of actions.

8. There can be borderline cases. When one says of the Japanese general whose campaign was disastrous that he killed himself in the traditional way, one seemingly merely reports a particular act, but in fact one does so in a manner laden with descriptive implications for other events.

9. At any rate, up to a point.

10. Anthony Kenny, *Action, Emotion, and Will* (London: Routledge & Kegan Paul, 1963).

11. Ibid., 160.

12. This chapter draws on Nicholas Rescher, "Aspects of Action," in *The Logic of Decision and Action,* ed. Nicholas Rescher (Pittsburgh, Pa.: University of Pittsburgh Press, 1967), 215–19.

Chapter 5

1. W. S Jevons, *The Principles of Science,* 2d ed. (London: Macmillan, 1877), 759.

2. The progress of science offers innumerable illustrations of this phenomenon, as does the process of individual maturation: "After three or thereabouts, the child begins asking himself and those around him questions, of which the most frequently noticed are the 'why' questions. By studying what the child asks 'why' about one can begin to see what kind of answers or solutions the child expects to receive. . . . A first general observation is that the child's whys bear witness to an intermediate precausality between the efficient cause and the final cause. Specifically, these questions seek reasons for phenomena which we see as fortuitous but which in the child arouse a need for a finalist explanations. 'Why are there two Mount Salèves, a big one and a little one?' asked a six-year-old boy. To which many of his contemporaries, when asked the same question, replied, 'One for big trips and another for small trips.'" Jean Piaget and B. Inhelder, *The Psychology of the Child,* trans. H. Weaver (New York: Basic Books, 1969), 109–10.

3. Immanuel Kant, *Prolegomena to Any Future Metaphysic* (1783), sec. 57, Akad., p. 352. Emphasis added.

4. Jevons, *Principles of Science,* 753.

5. Ibid.

6. Compare the discussion in Adolf Grünbaum, "Can a Theory Answer More Questions than One of Its Rivals?" *British Journal for the Philosophy of Science* 27 (1976):1–22.

7. See Paul K. Feyerabend, *Against Method* (London: Humanities Press, 1975), 176.

8. Larry Laudan, "Two Dogmas of Methodology," *Philosophy of Science* 43 (1976):585–97. See also Lauden, *Progress and Its Problems* (Berkeley: University of California Press, 1978).

9. Jevons, *Principles of Science,* 754.

10. Compare Laudan, *Progress and Its Problems.*

11. A homely fishing analogy of Eddington's is useful here. He saw the experimentalists as akin to a fisherman who trawls nature with the net of his equipment for detection and observation. Now suppose (says Eddington) that a fisherman trawls the seas using a fishnet of two-inch mesh. Fish smaller than two inches will simply go uncaught, and those who analyze the catch will have an incomplete and distorted view of aquatic life. The situation in science is the same. Only by improving our observational means of trawling nature can such imperfections be mitigated. See A. S. Eddington, *The Nature of the Physical World* (New York: Macmillian, 1928).

12. D. A. Bromley et al., *Physics in Perspective,* student ed. (Washington, D.C.:NRC/NAS Publications, 1973), 16.

13. Recall Goethe's stricture: "*Natur hat weder Kern noch Schale, Alles ist sie mit einem Male.*"

14. The geographic exploration analogy is an old standby: "Science cannot keep on going so that we are always going to discover more and more new laws. . . . It is like the discovery of America—you only discover it once. The age in which we live is the age in which we are discovering the fundamental laws of nature, and that day will never come again." See Richard Feynman, *The Character of Physical Law* (Cambridge, Mass.: MIT Press, 1965), 172. See also Gunter Stent, *The Coming of the Golden Age* (Garden City, N.Y.: Natural History Press, 1969); and S. W. Hawkins, "Is the End in Sight for Theoretical Physics?" *Physics Bulletin* 32 (1981):15–17.

15. In this regard, E. P. Wigner seems altogether correct in reminding us, "that in order to understand a growing body of phenomena, it will be necessary to introduce deeper and deeper concepts into physics and that this development will not end by the discovery of the final and perfect concepts. I believe that this is true: we have no right to expect that our intellect can formulate perfect concepts for the full understanding of inanimate nature's phenomena." See E. P. Wigner, "The Limits of Science," *Proceedings of the American Philosophical Society* 94 (1950):424.

16. Marxist theoreticians take this view very literally—in the manner of Lenin's idea of the "inexhaustibility" of matter in *Materialism and Empirico-Criticism*. Purporting to inherit from Spinoza a thesis of the infinity of nature, they construe this to mean that any cosmology that denies the infinite spatial extension of the universe must be wrong.

17. "Remarks by David Bohm," in *Observation and Interpretation*, ed. Stephan Koerner (New York and London, 1957), 56. For a fuller development of Bohm's views on the "qualitative infinity of nature," see David Bohm, *Causality and Chance in Modern Physics* (London: Routledge and Paul, 1957).

18. "If by the 'infinite complexity of nature' is meant only the infinite multiplicity of the *phenomena* it contains, there is no bar to final success in theory making, since theories are not concerned with particulars as such. So too, if what is meant is only the infinite variety of natural phenomena . . . that too may be comprehended in a unitary theory." See David Bohm, "Scientific Revolutions for Ever?" *British Journal for the Philosophy of Science* 19 (1967):41. For a suggestive analysis of "the architecture of complexity," see Herbert A. Simon, *The Sciences of the Artificial* (Cambridge, Mass.: MIT Press, 1969).

19. The idea that our knowledge about the world reflects an *interactive* process, to which both the *object* of knowledge (the world) and the knowing *subject* (the inquiring mind) make essential and ultimately inseparable contributions, is elaborated in Nicholas Rescher, *Conceptual Idealism* (Oxford: Blackwell, 1973).

20. Compare D. A. Bromley's observation: "Even if physicists could be sure that they had identified all the particulars that can exist, some obviously fundamental questions would remain. Why, for instance, does a certain universal ratio in atomic physics have the particular value 137.036 and not some other value? This is an experimental result: the precision of the experiments extends today to these six figures. Among other things, this number relates to the extent of size of the electron to the size of the atom, and that in turn to the wavelength of light emitted. From astronomical observation it is known that this fundamental ratio has the same numer-

ical value for atoms a billion years away in space and time. As yet there is no reason to doubt that other fundamental ratios, such as the ratio of the mass of the proton to that of the electron, are as uniform throughout the universe as is the geometrical ratio pi equals 3.14159. Could it be that such physical ratios are really, like pi, mathematical aspects of some underlying logical structure? If so, physicists are not much better off than people who must resort to wrapping a string around a cylinder to determine the value of pi! For theoretical physics thus far sheds hardly a glimmer of light on this question." D. A. Bromley et al., *Physics in Perspective*, 28.

21. See Nicholas Rescher, *Peirce's Philosophy of Science* (Notre Dame: University of Notre Dame Press, 1978).

22. The present critique of convergentism is thus very different from Quine's. He argues that the idea of "convergence to a limit" is defined for numbers but not for theories, so that speaking of scientific change as issuing in a "convergence to a limit" is a misleading metaphor. "There is a faulty use of mathematical analogy in speaking of a limit of theories, since the notion of a limit depends on that of a 'nearer than,' which is defined for numbers and not for theories." See Quine, *Word and Object*, 23. The metaphor of substantial and insignificant differences among theories makes perfectly good sense, but the idea that the course of scientific theory innovation must eventually descend to the level of trivialities certainly does not.

Chapter 6

1. The justification of such imputations is treated more fully in Nicholas Rescher, *Induction* (Oxford: Basil Blackwell, 1980), chap. 9.

2. The point is Kantian in its orientation. Kant holds that we cannot experientially learn through our perceptions about the objectivity of outer things, because we can only recognize our perceptions as perceptions (i.e., representations of outer things) if these outer things are given as such from the first (rather than being learned or inferred). As Kant summarizes in his "Refutation of Idealism": "Idealism assumed that the only

immediate experience is inner experience, and that from it we can only *infer* outer things—and this, moreover, only in an untrustworthy manner. . . . But on the above proof it has been shown that outer experience is really immediate." *Critique of Pure Reason,* B276.

3. Benedictus de Spinoza, *Ethics,* bk. 1, axiom 6.

4. Maimonides, *The Guide for the Perplexed,* I, 71, 96a.

Chapter 7

1. This objection was raised in Laurence BonJour, "Rescher's Idealistic Pragmatism," *Review of Metaphysics* 39 (1976):702–26.

2. This chapter draws on Nicholas Rescher, "Trapped within History," *Process Studies* 29 (2000): 66–76.

NAME INDEX